For unconditional feminist friends

Good Soldiers Don't Rape

Sexual violence is a significant problem within many Western militaries. Despite international attention to the issue and global #MeToo and #TimesUp movements highlighting the impact of sexual violence, rates of sexual violence are going up in many militaries. This book uses feminist theories of 'rape culture' and institutional gaslighting to identify the key stories, myths, and misconceptions about military sexual violence that have obstructed addressing and preventing it. It is a landmark study that considers nearly thirty years of media coverage of military sexual violence in three case countries – the US, Canada, and Australia. The findings have implications not only for those seeking to address, reduce, and prevent sexual violence in militaries, but also for those hoping to understanding rape culture and how patriarchy operates more broadly. It will appeal to students, scholars, and general readers interested in gender, feminism, and the military.

MEGAN MACKENZIE is one of the world's leading experts on gender and the military. Her book *Beyond the Band of Brothers: The US Military and the Myth That Women Can't Fight* (2015) was a landmark contribution that shaped debates on gender integration and military culture. Since then, she has led international studies on military suicide, sexual violence, and women in combat roles.

Good Soldiers Don't Rape

The Stories We Tell About Military Sexual Violence

MEGAN MACKENZIE

Simon Fraser University, British Columbia

CAMBRIDGE
UNIVERSITY PRESS

Shaftesbury Road, Cambridge CB2 8EA, United Kingdom

One Liberty Plaza, 20th Floor, New York, NY 10006, USA

477 Williamstown Road, Port Melbourne, VIC 3207, Australia

314–321, 3rd Floor, Plot 3, Splendor Forum, Jasola District Centre, New Delhi – 110025, India

103 Penang Road, #05–06/07, Visioncrest Commercial, Singapore 238467

Cambridge University Press is part of Cambridge University Press & Assessment, a department of the University of Cambridge.

We share the University's mission to contribute to society through the pursuit of education, learning and research at the highest international levels of excellence.

www.cambridge.org
Information on this title: www.cambridge.org/9781009273961

DOI: 10.1017/9781009273985

First published 2023

A catalogue record for this publication is available from the British Library.

Library of Congress Cataloging-in-Publication Data
Names: MacKenzie, Megan H. (Megan Hazel), author.
Title: Good soldiers don't rape : the stories we tell about military sexual violence / Megan MacKenzie, Simon Fraser University, British Columbia.
Other titles: Good soldiers do not rape
Description: Cambridge, United Kingdom ; New York, NY : Cambridge University Press, 2023. | Includes bibliographical references and index.
Identifiers: LCCN 2022050815 | ISBN 9781009273961 (hardback) |
ISBN 9781009273930 (paperback) | ISBN 9781009273985 (ebook)
Subjects: LCSH: Rape in the military – United States – Case studies. | Rape in the military – Canada – Case studies. | Rape in the military – Australia – Case studies. | Armed Forces and mass media – United States – Case studies. | Armed Forces and mass media – Canada – Case studies. | Armed Forces and mass media – Australia – Case studies. | Sexual harassment in the military – Prevention. | Rape culture.
Classification: LCC UB783 .M34 2023 |
DDC 362.88308835500973–dc23/eng/20230206
LC record available at https://lccn.loc.gov/2022050815

ISBN 978-1-009-27396-1 Hardback
ISBN 978-1-009-27393-0 Paperback

Contents

Figures

Acknowledgements

This damn book. I like to imagine writing books that are breezy, joyful, and that are written effortlessly while listening to music. Instead, I write about violence, militarism, and patriarchy through painful fits and starts, in silent stretches interrupted by my own loud exhales. Writing a book on sexual violence has been difficult, draining, and at times I needed to take significant breaks. To write this book I needed to read hundreds of articles about military sexual violence. Each of these articles shared a personal story of an event that forever changed someone's life for the worse. I'm an empath. Despite reading all the books about boundaries and attempting to draw lines around my work, I soaked up every single one of these stories as if they were water being absorbed into a thick coat. By the end of the writing process the weight of the stories and my imaginary heavy coat kept me in bed some days.

And yet, I wanted to write this book; I needed to write this book. Why start the acknowledgements this way? I want to make it clear that this project was important to me, and difficult. To write this book I didn't just need time and funding and space (though those were important). I needed feminist friends to go for a walk with me and despair together about the patriarchy. I needed my partner to insist I turn the light off, and get outdoors and out of the house during the last weeks of writing. I needed my colleagues and friends to assure me that although the early drafts were rough – and I am a terrible copyeditor – I was onto something. I needed my child to toddle into my bedroom as I sat at my desk staring at the screen to say 'Mom, is this book really a year overdue?'

I want to begin by thanking the team of researchers that helped me with this work. In particular, Eda Gunaydin and Umeya Chaudhuri began as undergrad research assistants in 2016 and our working relationship developed into one of co-authors. They both brought so much insight and brilliance to this project and were key to establishing the methods in the early days. Thanks also to the team of scholars and students that conducted work for this book as part of a 'pop up research lab' at the University of Sydney, including Harry Mayer, Matilda Stewart, Jackie Dent, Chris Hall, and Shannon Sampert. Special thanks to Maya Hibbeln for her excellent research and editing work and to Loren Aytona Arena who created the fantastic graphics and helped me visualize my work. Thank you also to John Haslam and the team at Cambridge University Press.

Thank you to those that read early drafts of the book and offered encouraging and engaging feedback, including Ken MacLeish, Nicole Wegner, Maya Eichler, Ben Wadham, Claire Duncanson, Laura Shepherd, Dean Cooper-Cunningham, Patricia Owens, Lene Hansen, Matthias Humer, and Simon Polichinel von der Maase. Thank you to colleagues at the University of Sydney and Simon Fraser University for listening to me present different elements of this work. Special thanks to Cait Hamilton for her excellent skills at editing and offering expert feedback on how to make my writing better.

This book is dedicated to unconditional feminist friends because they were key to making this project possible. I cherish my unconditional feminist friends, who are here for long discussions about sexism, rape culture, and the patriarchy and push me to be brave and finish the damn book. Special shout out to Ellen Haring and Toni Ricco for all our supportive long talks over the years as well as our endless group chats about the band of bros.

Nothing is more important to me than my family. Thank you to my children, for wonderful interruptions and reminding me that life is more important than deadlines. Thank you, Jason for being my unconditional feminist life partner and for bringing joy and lightness to our wild but beautiful life journey together.

Introduction

The title of this book – *Good Soldiers Don't Rape* – is a provocation, and one that is designed to dislocate and unsettle commonly-held beliefs about military sexual violence. There are multiple widely accepted, and almost taken for granted, stories about this kind of violence, including that its perpetrators are 'bad apples' and that militaries have zero tolerance for it. The problem is that this isn't the case.

For over a decade, my research has focused on military culture, the integration of women into militaries, military suicide, and sexual violence in the military. As a researcher, I have found it useful to begin my analysis by pinpointing unsettling or disruptive statements, and then exploring the series of beliefs, narratives, and norms that make such statements uncomfortable and disruptive. For example, in my previous work I have used statements like 'women can fight,' and 'combat is for sissies' (Encloe, 2011) as a starting point for a deeper analysis of a range of issues related to combat units and military culture. The core motivation for my work is to unravel key myths and logics that sustain and make war possible and palatable. I am interested in the stories we tell about war, the military, and military culture that smooth over what seem to be inconsistencies and contradictions related to war and militarism. In my research, for example, I have explored the stories we tell about female soldiers to resolve the former inconsistency between the policies that excluded women from serving in combat roles and the evidence that women had been regularly serving in combat for decades.

Another contradiction or inconsistency that has fascinated me for a number of years relates to military sexual violence (MSV), a term I use to refer to unwanted sexual activity perpetrated against service members by a fellow service member or members (MacKenzie, Gunaydin and Chaudhuri, 2020). Militaries are the most trusted public institution in most western countries and are often defined by order, discipline, and codes of honour – and yet there is clear evidence of disorder, indiscipline, and broken codes of honour in relation to internal sexual violence.

1

For example, in Australia, female service members have a one in four chance of being harassed or assaulted over the course of their career (Australian Human Rights Commission, 2013). Between 2016 and 2018, the US military saw a 38 per cent increase in cases of sexual assault (Philipps, 2019), and in July 2019, the Canadian government announced that it would pay nearly CAD $1 billion to members of the military who were part of a class action lawsuit claiming systemic and widespread sexual misconduct in the Canadian Defence Forces (Connolly, 2021). Nearly 19,000 Canadian Armed Forces and Defence personnel submitted claims as part of this Canadian class action lawsuit (Gallant, 2021). There is strong evidence that available data on MSV is merely the tip of the iceberg; research from several countries indicates that over 80 per cent of victims do not report their assault (Mulrine, 2012; DART, 2016, p. 31). Available data and research show that sexual violence committed by service members against fellow service members is pervasive and rampant in most western militaries. However, this evidence, and even high-profile cases or scandals, does not seem to tarnish military reputations or impact public trust.

Military sexual violence affects victims deeply and can have complex and long-term impacts on the health and well-being of victims. Sexual violence is associated with pregnancy and gynaecological complications, sexually transmitted diseases, an increased risk of suicide and suicide ideation, post-traumatic stress, career interruption, and social ostracization. Besides the significant and deep impacts of this violence on individuals, there are massive institutional and public costs associated with MSV. While it might seem insensitive to talk about financial costs related to MSV, militaries across the globe spend millions of dollars every year to settle sexual abuse claims. Between 2017 and 2020 Australia spent $50 million on sexual abuse claims from the (Wilson, 2020). Although it is difficult to secure an accurate figure, it has been estimated that the costs of addressing the health impacts of sexual assault on US veterans at $872 million (Francis, 2013). In addition to the costs of settling claims, there are a number of direct and indirect 'costs' associated with MSV, including the costs associated with investigations, training, victim support, recruitment to replace service members, and time off work due to injury, mental health, or for disciplinary measures.

In addition to these statistics, I am compelled to do this work by the personal testimonies that people have shared with me, and existing scholarship which reminds us that public conversations about sexual violence are always about more than just sexual violence. My work is inspired by feminist scholars who argue that the enactment of sexual violence should not merely be understood as 'incidents' but instead as 'wide-ranging constellations of behaviours, attitudes, beliefs, and talk that work to produce and reproduce gendered dominance in everyday interaction' (Hollander, 2015). Conversations about sexual violence also signal deep commitments and beliefs related to gender, race, and social order (Sielke, 2002; Benedict, 1992).

0.1 Making Sense of Military Sexual Violence

At the heart of this book, then, lies a contradiction: military sexual violence has been persistent, predictable, and proven. Yet, we nonetheless see the continuation of long-standing depictions of militaries as trusted and disciplined institutions that have a unique culture of camaraderie and protection. The reason why this is the case, I argue, is that there are a number of compelling stories and myths about MSV – stories that we need to study in order to understand how the public comes to make sense of, and normalize, MSV. To do this, I have analysed nearly 30 years of media coverage of MSV across three case countries: Australia, Canada, and the US. My goal has been to identify overarching stories, or narratives, which have been told about MSV, as well as the rhetorical tools used to help convey the problem of MSV.

I have had to be thoughtful about how I write about MSV. It is such a sensitive and personal subject. I thought long and hard about if and how to include personal stories, narratives, and victim perspectives in the book. Personal stories and testimonials are a powerful way to illustrate the impact and significance of this issue. However, the emphasis of this book is on public conversations about MSV – focussed on media coverage – and, accordingly, how the public has come to make sense of MSV as a systemic problem. This is not just an academic analysis; it is about holding ourselves accountable to how we talk about (and have talked about) this issue.

I am also still unsure as to how (and if) victim/survivor stories can be brought into an academic text in a way that is consensual, ethical, and productive, rather than extractive. Over the course of my career, several service members have disclosed to me incidents of sexual violence that they have experienced, witnessed, or had to deal with as a commander. In fact, there are few women service members I have spoken with who have *not* directly experienced, witnessed, and supported others coping with sexual violence. According to the ethics guidelines and consent forms I used as part of this process, I could technically bring those stories into this book; however, I don't do so for several reasons. First, the overall focus of this book is on public conversations about MSV. While survivor stories can help readers understand the gravity of this issue and its complex effects, I want the attention to be squarely focused on holding the public accountable to our patterns of making sense of this problem. In some ways, emphasizing individual stories risks shifting attention from the broader patterns I seek to illustrate.

Second, as a feminist I think it is necessary to be extremely conscious of the ways that testimonials related to sexual violence and assault are shared and 'used.' A key aspect of sexual assault is the violation of consent. Feminists have worked to shift the definition of consent from 'no means no' towards an understanding of enthusiastic and ongoing consent. This means that in a sexual encounter, the onus is not merely on the victim to say 'no' to what they do not want; rather, the onus is on all individuals to ensure an encounter is consensual and pleasurable throughout.

I wonder what enthusiastic and continuous consent might mean in a research context? It seems to me that it requires researchers to do more than just ask participants to sign a consent form. Participants might share something in an interview or interaction that they feel differently about after the interview, or even years later. It is reasonable to assume that survivors might shift their perspectives and that life events and a myriad of factors could impact their original consent. Enthusiastic and ongoing consent to sensitive and personal stories requires that we continually check in with participants and ensure that they are comfortable with what they have shared and with how we are considering drawing on their stories for our work.

Again, while I do think survivor stories are important to understanding this issue, I'm not sure how to fulfill my commitment to feminist ethics of consent when writing a book; publishing a survivor's story when they cannot later revise or retract it is not something I feel comfortable with. This is one of the reasons the #MeToo movement has been so powerful: it is a movement driven in part by survivors sharing their stories on their own terms. Survivors should be in control of their stories, and while it would be a valuable project, this book is not focussed on working with survivors to present their perspectives. That would be an entirely different project.

Similarly, in the course of my scholarship and through my public engagement work on MSV, I am often asked about my own positionality and my decision not to centre the voices of victims of MSV. While I appreciate feminist calls for scholars to situate themselves in their work, I resist the expectation for women to validate their work related to sexual violence and patriarchy by revealing personal details and instances of deep vulnerability. It has been necessary for me to set boundaries for both myself and for this project to make it possible to do the work. One of those boundaries is not having to legitimize my ability to conduct this work by disclosing personal experiences I do not want to share. While personal stories are important to movements to end sexual violence and resist patriarchy, the demand for victim testimonies or researchers' personal experiences reflects a misogynist desire to sensationalize sexual violence and focus on the personal rather than the systemic nature of sexual violence and how rape culture operates.

I'm also aware of 'trauma porn' and the ways that the public can become fixated on the salacious details of an individual case, sometimes at the expense of observing broader political patterns. In the wake of #MeToo and the sharing of stories, there is a sense that personal testimonials are the only way to push political change. Talking about the #MeToo hashtag and the many survivors that came forward with their stories, Tarana Bourke, the founder of the movement, warned, 'We should be careful that people don't turn our stories into fodder for their trauma porn' (quoted in Wulfhorst 2019). She also noted 'there's power in not telling your story.' (2019)With all this in mind, I chose to focus on media coverage of MSV rather than drawing on interviews or focusing merely on statistics and data.

0.2 Analysing Media Coverage of Military Sexual Violence

An analysis of media coverage is useful in exploring how the public comes to make sense of MSV and the stories that are told about MSV for several reasons. First, media coverage is one of the primary sources of information the public has about military affairs, and public narratives about MSV are both shaped by and reflected in media coverage. Government and defence forces also respond to, and use, media outlets strategically. Andrews et al. argue that military organizations manage public attention and scrutiny strategically in order to 'maximiz[e] the benefits of eliciting positive public attention while minimizing the consequences that can arise from negative public attention' (Andrews, Connor and Wadham, 2020, p. 271). My analysis shows that what we know about MSV is political, limited, and largely shaped by high-profile incidents that garner significant media attention. I demonstrate a clear 'call and response' relationship between media coverage of MSV and government and military official responses to this issue. Studying media coverage of MSV sheds light on the relationship between media coverage and political responses and illuminates the patterns and the narratives that emerge through this coverage.

A second reason that analysing media is useful is that media coverage of civilian sexual violence has found that public narratives have historically been shaped by gender bias and what researchers call 'rape myths', or 'prejudicial, stereotyped, or false beliefs about rape, rape victims, and rapists' (Burt, 1980, p. 270). Specific rape myths in the civilian context include versions of 'she was asking for it', 'women often lie', and 'good guys don't rape'. These rape myths have significant impacts. Researchers have found that when rape myths are accepted, there are increased negative perceptions of rape survivors (Lonsway and Fitzgerald, 1994), lower conviction rates and shorter sentences for perpetrators (Finch and Munro, 2004), and police reports that reproduce rape myths (Shaw et al., 2017). Analysing media coverage of sexual violence can provide insights into the stories we tell about sexual violence and how these stories are political, impactful, and often shaped by gender bias. While there is significant work exploring rape myths in media coverage of civilian sexual violence, there has not been a similar analysis of media coverage of MSV across multiple cases. As a result, we know very little about the stories told about MSV or whether there are particular MSV rape myths, or dominant narratives and rhetorical tools specific to coverage of MSV. This book addresses this gap.

The central argument I put forward in this book is that there are persistent gendered narratives in media coverage of MSV, which are salient over time and have come to form part of public common understandings of the problem. Building on work exploring 'rape myths', this book focusses on the dominant narratives and rhetorical tools used in media coverage to convey messages about, make sense of, and smooth out contradictions related to MSV. I am inspired by existing work on rape myths; however, my analysis departs from this scholarship both theoretically and in my methodological approach. The literature on rape myths takes a somewhat narrow approach to defining myths as 'untruths', or misperceptions; in contrast, my goal is not to identify myths understood as factually incorrect beliefs.

Instead, I am interested in identifying the stories we tell about MSV and exploring the ways that these stories may close out space for alternative ways of making sense of MSV and may inhibit action or systemic change that could reduce MSV. Through my analysis, I find that MSV is consistently presented as either a problem already being solved, a problem so endemic that it cannot be solved, or not a problem at all and therefore not requiring solving. I argue the narratives and rhetoric unite with a singular message of justified inaction. The narratives I identify, as well as the overarching message that 'nothing can/should be done', helps answer the core question of this book. I argue that narratives found in media coverage of MSV illustrate how the public comes to normalize, accept, and diminish the problem of MSV while upholding ideals of military exceptionalism, and reverence for 'good soldiers.'

In doing so, I draw heavily from the work of Sherene Razack, who argues that case study analysis and attention to the construction and articulation of national mythologies is illustrative of how power, sexism, and racism operate within a society. In her work on Canadian soldier atrocities in Somalia, Razack reminds us that 'the hold that mythologies have should not be underestimated. They have the power to make a nation replace tortured and dead bodies with traumatized soldiers. Mythologies help the nation to forget its bloody past and present' (2004, p. 9). Razack argues that work that draws out national myths and narratives is not only vital, but also potentially transformative; identifying national myths and rhetoric makes it possible to dismantle and move beyond these narratives to create space and alternative ways of envisioning and organizing society. (2004) My work on MSV is aimed at transformation and seeks to identify narratives and rhetoric associated with MSV to create space for dismantling, unravelling, and creating space for alternative visions of the military, the use of violence, and gendered orders.

0.3 Rape Culture

This analysis of how the public makes sense of MSV and how media coverage might serve to smooth out contradictions associated with sexual violence in the military feeds into broader global debates about rape culture and the implications of the #MeToo movement. In fact, the claim driving this book is that if we want to understand rape culture, we need to explore how and why the most trusted public institution in most countries – the military – maintains its revered status despite extensive evidence of rampant sexual violence.

The term 'rape culture' has been frequently used in the past decade yet is often loosely or poorly defined. Black feminists developed a clear understanding of rape culture as a masculine system of control that treats sexual and physical domination as an articulation of power and supremacy (Hill Collins, 2008). According to this understanding of rape culture, sexual violence is used not only to gain 'masculine capital,' but also to put those who are not deemed to be at the top of the hierarchy – particularly women and marginalized groups – 'in their place' (Bridges and Pascoe, 2014). In other words, sexual assault is both an articulation of masculine and white power, and a tool used to reinforce or recover hierarchies and power structures that position white men at the top. Expressions of sexual and physical violence are expressions of individual masculinity *and* expressions of national masculinity and supremacy at the same time.

By centring power and hierarchy, this definition of rape culture helps to explain how violence enacted by those understood to be at the top of the social hierarchy (white men) can be legitimized and even revered as a form of protection. In a rape culture, white male sexual violence is not a disruptive threat but can be viewed as sustaining the existing system. With this understanding of rape culture, it becomes urgent to study how sexual violence operates within national militaries. National militaries are heralded as exceptional and elite institutions. They are the most trusted public institution in most western countries and are presented as masculine institutions designed to protect a feminized nation. White soldiers working within militaries and defence are among the most privileged, revered, and elite subjects in a white supremacist, patriarchal, militarized society. Understanding how these service members enact violence, and how sexual violence is addressed or legitimized is therefore incredibly important to understand how patriarchy functions, as well as to any commitments to dismantling rape culture

Although I identify narratives and rhetoric that are distinct from rape myths about civilian sexual assault, I argue that the narratives and forms of rhetoric used in media coverage of MSV are similar to the rape myths associated with civilian sexual assault in that they create a series of excuses and rationales to help make sense of the violence in ways that tend to variously remove institutional accountability, evade the acknowledgement of a systemic and persistent institutional problem, and diffuse or weaken efforts to address the problem. My analysis of the commonalities and distinctions between narratives of sexual violence in the military reinforce existing work on sexual violence and extends this by showing how sexism, patriarchy, and militarism operate both within and outside of the military.

0.4 Military Exceptionalism and Institutional Gaslighting

I develop the concept of military exceptionalism to explain how evidence of MSV and regular scandals can become understood as acceptable and not requiring significant reform or attention. As I elaborate in Chapter 1, I understand military exceptionalism as more than just a term reflecting the uniqueness of the military. Grounded in Black Feminist work and feminist critical military scholarship, and particularly the work of Sherene Razack (2004), I argue that military exceptionalism is key to understanding how illicit behaviours committed by soldiers or military institution are rationalized and justified in public discourse. Military exceptionalism is shaped by ideals of 'good militaries' and 'good soldiers', which are constructed as necessarily white, masculine, exclusive, and reproduced through the regulation of sex and the exclusion of women and racialized groups. More so than other workplaces, military work is framed as a form of disciplined sacrifice that is extreme and worthy of reverence.

The concept of military exceptionalism captures the complex and sometimes paradoxical ways that 'good militaries' and 'good soldiers' are seen to be *both* disciplined protectors of the nation – exercising legitimate violence – *and* untameable and always capable of reasonable indiscipline and illegitimate violence. Through my analysis, I show how ideals of military institutions and culture presume *both* romantic notions of camaraderie, band of brother loyalty, hierarchy, and honourable masculinity *and* regular – often accepted – dysfunctional practices such as hazing and war crimes. Similarly, the 'good soldier' has been historically constructed *both* as a stoic, professional, and controlled man that follows orders *and* as an untamed warrior that occasionally – but understandably – 'comes undone', either as a result of being overcome by witnessing violence and the spectre of 'evil' in war zones (S. H. Razack, 2004), or from the burden of his role as defender of the nation.

I argue that the narratives and rhetorical tools I identify in media coverage of MSV essentially reveal how MSV is not only normalized to a public audience, but also how MSV can come to be understood as part of a 'good' military and the unfortunate but understandable actions of nevertheless 'good' soldiers. In turn, this type of narrative and rhetoric analysis sheds light not only on how military institutions respond to 'scandals' and diffuse negative public attention, but also on entrenched beliefs associated with military exceptionalism that legitimize dysfunction and violence.

In addition to military exceptionalism, I use the concept of institutional gaslighting to understand narratives of MSV. As I explain further in Chapter 1, gaslighting has typically referred to a practice used within intimate relationships to cause someone to question their sanity or perception of reality. I draw on Black feminist scholarship that has critiqued popular uses of the concept, which tend to focus on white women and their male partners, and ignore the multiple forms of oppression that might impact an individual's experience of being 'gaslit,' or made to feel irrelevant, irrational, and unable to narrate their own experience. Elena Ruiz, for example, argues this understanding of gaslighting '[i]s a settler conceptual ruse that diverts critical attention away from structural epistemic oppressions that continue to underwrite the colonial project' (Ruíz, 2020, p. 689). Ruiz argues that rather than just undermining women, or making them feel 'crazy,' gaslighting is an 'enduring process' aimed at sustaining existing power structures, including 'the maintenance, upkeep, and regeneration of white supremacy' (Ruíz, 2020, p. 693). Thus, gaslighting should be seen as a response to efforts to resist existing power structures. Institutional gaslighting includes political strategies to resist critiques of the institution or discredit evidence that undermines the authority or carefully crafted image of the institution. Kennedy-Cuomo argues that institutions – particularly trusted institutions such as universities and militaries – use a range of tactics to respond to any evidence that undermines their image, including distracting, trivializing, and denying (Kennedy-Cuomo, 2019). Drawing from this work, I treat narratives and rhetoric associated with MSV as forms of institutional gaslighting aimed at maintaining existing power structures and resisting attempts at meaningful reform of the institution.

Institutional gaslighting is not simply about denying that a social phenomenon exists, but rather about creating narratives about that phenomenon that render entire communities and their experiences irrelevant and disregarded. Seen in this way, the concept of institutional gaslighting becomes useful in analysing MSV rhetoric. In this project, I am not simply identifying MSV rhetoric and narratives to show their factual inaccuracies; rather, I use the concept of institutional gaslighting to explore the ways that MSV rhetoric may reinforce existing power dynamics and deny or erase experiences that could challenge carefully crafted images of the good military and good soldiers. In my analysis, I explore several ways that MSV rhetoric might operate as a form of institutional gaslighting.

My analysis does not pit institutional and public accounts of MSV against survivor accounts of MSV, nor does it situate narrative analysis as an 'alternative' to the available data we have about MSV. In fact, one of the secondary arguments I make is that MSV 'data' is not a more objective, clear, or accurate source of information about MSV compared to media analysis and storytelling about MSV. Rather, MSV statistics and data *are* stories told by institutions; they are shaped by what information is collected and made available, and what information is erased, ignored, or kept private. As I indicated above, my analysis is centred on rhetoric and public media coverage of MSV not as it compares to victim stories, but as a tool for understanding patterns, narratives, and rhetoric. This is an important distinction to make to better understand the methods I have chosen for this analysis.

0.5 Case Studies and Stages of Analysis

This book explores media coverage of MSV in Canada, Australia, and the US between 1991 and 2017. I selected these case study countries because all three have identified MSV as a significant and pressing political problem within their respective national defence forces, and all have faced a range of MSV 'scandals', or cases that garnered significant national and international attention. This allows for an analysis of the patterns of media coverage associated with such scandals and 'lulls'. I examined the top four print news outlets in each case study country with attention to any articles that focused explicitly on MSV, or intra-service sexual violence.

As I will explain in greater detail in Chapter 1, there were several stages to the analysis. First, I conducted a framing analysis aimed at identifying themes, general patterns over time, and distinctions between cases. The framing analysis was a useful first step to grasping the content of the articles and observing general trends. The second stage of analysis was aimed at identifying overarching narratives and rhetorical tools. Drawing on the work of Laura Shepherd, I treat narratives as complete, consistent, and often familiar stories told to make sense and offer explanations of political and social events. A narrative is not simply a story; it is a widely recognized and regularly reproduced account that is aimed at rationalizing, validating, or describing complex phenomena in a coherent and definitive manner (2009). I treat narratives as stabilizing forces; they are the through line that emerges through multiple articulations of a problem or issue. In addition to focusing on narratives, I also identify a number of rhetorical tools, which are language tactics, strategies, and techniques consistent over time and used to persuade.

0.6 Main Findings

I think it is helpful to signal some of the key findings here, before elaborating on these in the chapters that follow. As indicated, the first stage of my analysis involved identifying themes and dominant frames in media articles. The goal of this stage was to highlight patterns that exist in the media coverage both over time and across case countries. Figure 0.1 signals the main themes identified in media coverage and their distribution across the countries. This visual shows that media coverage was dominated by five themes: military justice, a focus on the structure of the institution, culture, gender/gender integration, and change. What I found fascinating about this visual, is that it captures how nearly 30 years of media coverage is dominated by a very small number of topics.

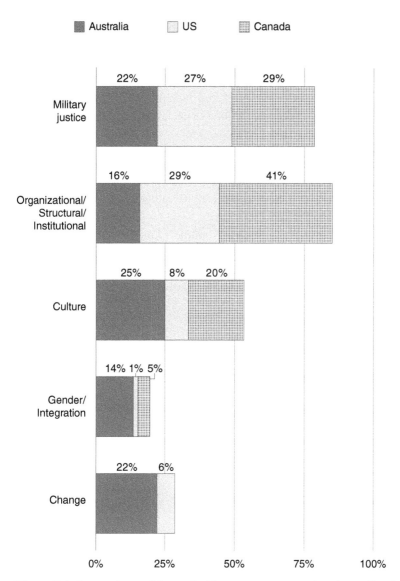

Figure 0.1 Comparison of frame incidence across countries: Australia, the United States and Canada.

I also note that gender is a relatively minor focus throughout media coverage, with attention to court cases seeming to dominate over the majority of the coverage.

In the second stage of analysis, I identify several consistent narratives, or stories told about MSV for each case study country. Below, I list the titles I gave to each of the dominant narratives, which give a sense of the stories that I explore in greater detail in each of the chapters. While these titles are brief and lacking context, they provide a hint of the analysis that will follow in each chapter.

0.7 US Media Narratives

1. The Band of Brothers invoke the 'bro code' and get away with MSV.
2. The military is a hostile place for women, and victims of MSV should know that.
3. If you want strong 'warrior' soldiers, not a bunch of wimps, expect MSV.
4. Women lie to ruin good men's honourable careers.
5. MSV is an issue that has been overblown by people who just don't 'get it'.

0.8 Canada Media Narratives

1. MSV is a complex problem that takes time to address.
2. MSV is a systemic force of nature.
3. MSV is a source of embarrassment for an institution we should be proud of.
4. The military is a 'boys' club' and not a place for women.

0.9 Australia Media Narratives

1. Drinking is an essential part of military culture and can lead to sexual assaults.
2. Military culture is admirable and dysfunctional.
3. Women shouldn't be in the military and men can't be expected to control their urges.
4. Everything is OK because we're committed to change.

In addition to identifying these country-specific narratives, I explore three overarching narratives that were consistent across all three case countries. In Chapter 7 I describe these three meta narratives, which I argue signal a potential western consensus on how MSV is understood.

0.10 Overarching Narratives

1. There are essential elements to military culture that lead to MSV.
2. The public does not understand the nature of the problem of MSV.
3. Militaries are hostile institutions for women.

While much of this book is focused on narratives, I also isolate a series of rhetorical tools. Rhetorical tools are distinct because they are not consistent or complete stories, but rather linguistic strategies – including catchphrases, strategic use of data or interviews, and overt political claims – used consistently to convince and convey a particular message. In Chapter 7, I identify the following six dominant forms of MSV rhetoric:

1. Calls for more evidence.
2. Referencing the service record of the accused or the victim.
3. Referencing the reputational damage of MSV allegations to the military institution.
4. Citing a previous government's failure to address MSV.
5. Zero tolerance statements.
6. Statement of support from women.

What unites these narratives and rhetorical tools is that they disrupt the idea that MSV is a systemic issue that requires dedicated solutions. MSV is consistently made sense of as a problem which is already in the process of being solved, an engrained problem that cannot be solved, or not a problem at all, the effect of which is to legitimate inaction around the issue of MSV.

0.11 More than a 'Military Problem'

MSV is more than just a 'military problem'; studying it matters not only because it impacts victims and survivors, but also because the stories we tell about MSV help us to understand deeply-held beliefs about militarism, gender, sexism, and national identity. MSV is the eye of the storm when it comes to rape culture and understanding sexual violence in the military is at the heart of unpacking rape culture. Military institutions are revered and held as models for society. They are also positioned as the masculine 'protector' of social order and seen as essential for maintaining political order and protecting freedoms. Given this reverence, and the ways that this institution is positioned as the 'father' of social order, that there is persistent sexual violence within these institutions should spark feminist curiosity. We can better understand and address rape culture if we face the deep contradiction that militaries remain highly trusted and revered public institutions in most Western countries – purportedly characterized by discipline and strict honour codes – despite evidence that sexual violence has been widespread, persistent, predictable, and woefully managed in the military for decades.

Linking research on MSV to the broader conversations on rape culture – international movements that highlight misogyny and sexual assault, such as #MeToo and #TimesUp – is important because, up to this point, MSV has been largely left out of international discussions of gender-based violence, sexual assault and abuse, and academic work on sexual violence and rape culture. Despite evidence that it is a regular and predictable problem across many national militaries, this evidence has not translated into MSV being brought into the fold of wider efforts to address, understand, and reduce sexual violence. For example, the United Nations' *Women, Peace and Security Agenda* aims to reduce international gender-based violence and exploitation; and variations of the #MeToo and #TimesUp movements have raised awareness about sexual harassment and abuse in a number of industries. However, these efforts have largely overlooked sexual violence that occurs *within* national militaries (Rico, 2017). In addition, the established body of academic literature theorizing and examining sexual violence, rape culture, and rape myths is largely focused on civilians, and in the context of MSV, is primarily centred on case studies, 'scandals', and limited empirical data.

The result of leaving MSV out of such important advancements in research related to sexual violence is that there are significant gaps in public knowledge about MSV. In particular, not enough is understood about how the public makes sense of widespread and consistent evidence of the prevalence of MSV in most military institutions. In short, we know little about how we talk about MSV. It is important to understand how we speak about MSV and how the media covers this issue. Public conversations about sexual violence are political and always about more than just sexual violence: they signal deeply held beliefs about gender, power, and social order. The fact that we know so little about MSV, including patterns in public narratives about MSV, not only restricts our understanding of the unique nature of MSV, but also limits efforts to create effective responses and solutions to reduce MSV.

In Chapter 1, I detail the theoretical concepts and methods used throughout the book. This is followed by Chapter 2, focussed on definitions and defining scandals of MSV. This chapter explains how each of the case study countries has defined and responded to MSV over the past several decades and also summarizes some of the defining scandals (or high-profile cases of MSV) for each country. The three chapters that follow – Chapters 3, 4 and 5 – focus on each of the case countries. I begin these chapters with a discussion of unique elements of the national context, before I explore the frames and narratives identified in media coverage for that country. Chapter 6 then examines the six rhetorical tools identified across all three case study countries and provides a deeper analysis of zero tolerance statements and statements of support for women. In the Conclusion, I draw out what I see as the meta trends to media coverage of MSV in these countries and outline what I consider to be necessary guidelines for media coverage of MSV in the future.

1 | *Military Exceptionalism*

1.1 Introduction

This chapter outlines the original theoretical contributions of the book: my development of the concepts of military exceptionalism and institutional gaslighting, and my examination of Military Sexual Violence (MSV) rhetoric. The main theoretical claim I make is that military exceptionalism is an organizing concept useful for understanding how the stories we tell about MSV can both gaslight attempts to demonstrate that MSV is a systemic problem and smooth out the contradictions associated with MSV. I unpack each element of this claim in the sections below, beginning by exploring the concept of military exceptionalism. I argue that this idea captures the intricate and expansive ways that the military is understood to be not only 'special' but also not accountable to civilian standards and laws. I then clarify my use of the term 'institutional gaslighting,' arguing that MSV narratives and rhetoric can operate to erase, diminish, and disparage attempts to describe MSV as a systemic problem, while reinforcing and salvaging perceptions of the military as a protective, honourable, and elite institution.

1.2 Black Women and Black Feminists Are Experts on Structural Sexual Violence

My theoretical contributions are indebted to Black feminist scholarship, particularly Black feminists situated in the US. One of the goals of this book is to develop further knowledge about how the public makes sense of MSV, understood as a form of structural violence. Any genuine effort to understand sexual violence should take seriously the perspectives of Black women, who have privileged knowledge of sexual violence because of the history of the use of sexual violence within white settler societies as well as Black women's long-standing

18

resistance to this violence. Black feminists have drawn attention to how sexual violence against Black women has been a tool of white domination and suppression – including during slavery and the civil rights movement, and as evidenced by ongoing inaction and apathy related to missing and murdered Indigenous women, and violence towards migrants and domestic workers (Razack, 2016; McGuire, 2011).

Black women have also led efforts to resist, politicize and gather knowledge about sexual violence. As Nora Berenstain points out, 'as long as Black women in the US have experienced sexual violence, they have engaged in interpretive practices of theorizing and resisting it' (Berenstain, 2020, p. 743). Black women were among the first to identify sexual harassment as an illegal form of sex discrimination. High-profile plaintiffs in sexual assault and harassment cases like Diane Williams, Paulette Barnes, Mechelle Vinson, Sandra Bundy, and Anita Hill raised public awareness of sexual harassment at significant personal expense (Berenstain, 2020). Black feminists have also highlighted how race shapes who is understood to be a sexual violence perpetrator and victim. Patricia Hill Collins argues that white women are more easily seen as fragile victims deserving of protection, while Black women 'have tended to be portrayed as promiscuous, sexually insatiable, and animalistic in their sexuality' (Collins, 2000, p. 123). Similarly, Black men have been hypersexualized and more readily presumed to be guilty of sexual violence – particularly against white female bodies. In contrast, white men are permitted space to express 'accepted' rage and 'legitimate' violence. The implications of this racism are stark: Black men are more likely to be wrongfully convicted of sexual assault and face longer sentences for assault than white men, while Black women are more likely to be victims of rape than white women, and often face re-victimization from the judicial system (Hale and Matt, 2019).

Black feminists have resisted white and Western feminist tendencies to examine gendered issues like rape or sexual violence in isolation from structured forms of social oppression. Black feminists, such as bell hooks, have demanded that feminism be defined not merely as a 'lens' or a curiosity that draws our attention to some 'women's issues,' but as a movement to end patriarchy by paying attention to the interconnectedness of white supremacy, patriarchy, capitalism, and militarism (bell hooks, 2000). Refusing to separate sexual violence from other forms of structural violence, Black feminists point to how sexual

violence is used to signal masculinity, supremacy, and national power
(Ruíz, 2020). In her work on soldier atrocities, Sherene Razack explicitly connects the racial and gendered nature of this violence, arguing
that such acts 'convince men of their own masculine and racial superi-
ority' (Razack, 2004, p. 10). Similarly, Patricia Hill Collins describes
hegemonic masculinity as predicated on the sexual and physical domination of women, while Tristan Bridges and C.J. Pascoe argue acts of
domination provide men with a form of social and masculine 'capital'
(Bridges and Pascoe, 2014). Drawing from this work, I treat sexual
violence as one of many forms of violence used to reinforce a gendered and racialised hierarchy that imagines white men as supreme. In
most Western countries militaries and soldiers are revered and understood to be central to maintaining order. As a result of their elite and
exceptional status, sexual violence perpetrated both by and within the
military can become normalized as a legitimate expression of power,
supremacy, domination, and masculine nationalism. In section 1.3,
I explore the ideal of military exceptionalism in greater detail.

1.3 Military Exceptionalism

Military exceptionalism is a term that tends to refer to the unique
nature of military service, and the esteemed place that the military
holds within society and the public imagination. Military exceptionalism is often only loosely defined; it is associated with the assumption that militaries are, and should be, subject to different standards
and forms of accountability compared to civilians. This vague definition of military exceptionalism defies Black feminist calls to examine
how militarism, patriarchy, and racism intersect. I argue that military
exceptionalism is more than just a term reflecting the uniqueness of the
military; rather, grounded in Black feminist work and feminist critical
military scholarship, I argue that military exceptionalism is shaped by
ideals of 'good militaries' and 'good soldiers' which are constructed as
necessarily white and masculine (Wadham, 2017).

Many workplaces – such as hospital emergency rooms – might be
described as extraordinary or extreme; however, there seems to be a
widely accepted understanding that national militaries are *more* exceptional and exceptional in ways that distinguish them from other workplaces. My argument here does not concern whether militaries are or
are not unique, but rather considers how militaries are *described* in

ways that separate them from other workplaces and presume a level of exceptionalism that puts militaries in a category of their own. Military institutions are often depicted as special and inherently 'good' institutions due their unique design, internal processes and traditions, and the types of activities and work that service members are trained and expected to do. More so than other workplaces, military work is framed as a form of disciplined sacrifice that is extreme and worthy of reverence. The work of service members tends to be framed as a form of sacrifice made on behalf of their fellow civilians (Millar and Tidy, 2017). The training, working conditions, and deployments and missions that service members undertake all reinforce perceptions of service members as disciplined and committed to a common purpose. Moreover, the very objectives of military institutions are associated with providing order and protection to civilians (Young, 2003).

In addition to the unique mission and work conditions, the 'good military' in the US, Canada, and Australia has historically been defined, at least in part, by both the regulation of sex and the unique bonds of all-white, all-male units. The regulation of sex, including strict codes and rules related to fraternization, adultery, and consensual relationships between soldiers are central to ideals of military sacrifice, burden, and exceptionalism that define the 'good military.' In her 2014 article, Carolyn Warner compares military institutions to the Catholic church in terms of how public awe and devotion to the institution is connected to sexual regulation and the ways in which both institutions have consistently been publicly – and institutionally – absolved of responsibility for persistent evidence of sexual abuse (Warner, 2014).

'Good militaries' are also defined by romantic notions of a 'band of brother' military culture featuring all-male units that are uniquely bonded in ways that allow them to defend the nation and serve in wars effectively (MacKenzie, 2015; Wadham, 2013, 2017). Establishing a unique military group culture is described as a key goal of a boot camp. Initiations and hazing continue to be reinforced through group expectations, rituals, and bonding activities that can put pressure on soldiers to participate or face exclusion (Higate, 2012). All-male units have been sustained by military policies limiting or restricting racialized men and women from certain positions, particularly combat and special forces roles (Barno and Bensahel, 2020). Historically, it was assumed that Black men and women spoiled soldierly bonding and weakened unit cohesion. Moreover, hazing and initiation rituals have been found to uniquely target racialized men and women, present-ing them as spoilers, outsiders, or weak links. In sum, the veneration of white men is central to ideals of the 'good' military, as are long-standing practices of racism, sexism, and the legitimate use of violence towards those deemed 'outsiders.'

In addition to the ideal of the 'good military,' at the heart of ideals about military exceptionalism is an idealized 'good soldier' that is hyper-masculine and white male (Wadham, 2013). There are slight variations of the ideal 'good soldier,' particularly depending on national context and type of military service; however, there are con-sistent elements that render the 'good soldier' a complex and well-established ideal type that reflects deeply held assumptions about war, masculinity, and service. The first of these elements is that 'good soldiers' are often assumed to be men. Most of the qualities associated with service members and soldiering – notions of bravery, stoicism, strength, and physical power – are gendered masculine and more readily assumed to be characteristics men can fulfil (see Duncanson, 2013; Duriesmith, 2017; Eichler, 2014). David Marlowe, former Chief of Military Psychiatry at the Walter Reed Army Institute of Research summarizes this ideal as follows: 'The soldier's world is characterised by a stereotyped masculinity. His language is profane, his professed sexuality crude and direct; his maleness is his armour, the measures of his competence, capability, and confidence in himself' (Carreiras, 2006).

It is not simply the case that ideal soldiers are male and mascu-line; there is evidence that militaries actively and persistently diminish and devalue anything associated with femininity, including women. Both the integration of women and qualities traditionally associated with femininity – including softness, compassion, and sensitivity – are depicted as forms of 'threats' to the military. Scholars have noted insti-tutional anxiety about 'feminization' within the armed forces (Titunik, 2008), and how some service members understand the integration of women and efforts to address systemic sexism as 'castrating' the military (MacKenzie, 2015). There are also instances across multiple militaries of male soldiers being insulted or degraded by being called 'women' or being described with terms associated with femininity or homosexuality. Randy Shills explains, 'calling [male] recruits as "ladies" or "girls" "faggots, sissies, pussies, and girls" had been a time-honoured strategy for drill instructors throughout the armed forces.

The context was clear; there was not much worse you could call a man' (Shilts, 1994, p. 133). Similarly, (Morris, 1995) recounts how training slides for the US Marines historically used the term 'Suzie Rottencrotch' to refer to women (Morris, 1995). Madeline Morris quotes one training slide, which stated, 'Privates, if you don't have a little Suzie now, maybe you're going to find one woman when you get home. You bet. You'll find the first cheap slut when you can get back home.' In his recent work on military culture in Australia, Ben Wadham outlined rampant evidence of misogyny and antagonism towards women (Wadham, 2017). In sum, the ideal of the 'good' soldier is not simply associated with a tough masculine male subject, but by an open hostility to femininity and women.

The 'good' soldier also represents the national character and embodies gendered and racialized values that render white able-bodied men as the most esteemed members of society, and the presumed protectors of the nation (Wadham, 2017). Mason, uses the concept of the 'hillbilly defense' to illustrate how 'good' small-town American soldiers are portrayed as humble, stoic, 'noble in poverty, pure in intentions' while dysfunctional or 'bad' soldiers are cast as 'hillbillies' who are 'innately violent, and sexually wild'. (2005, 41) Whiteness is central to the construction of 'good' and 'bad' 'hillbilly'; white male soldiers are more readily associated with romantic notions of soldiers as small-town heroes. In addition, crimes or atrocities committed by white soldiers seem to be more readily excused as exceptional, the result of 'bad apples,' or the product of soldier trauma. White soldiers are given greater liberty to express rage, to make mistakes, and to be 'out of control' and still hold the 'good soldier' title. In sum, the 'good' soldier is a complex idealized figure; a white hyper-masculine male who is romanticized and allowed to 'lose control' and express legitimized violence, and who rejects femininity and sees women as either spoilers or conquests.

Scholars like Raewyn Connell and Amira Silverman (Silverman, 2020) remind us that idealized notions of masculinity and masculine institutions are unattainable by design and require constant efforts to try to realize and articulate these ideals. Vandello and Silverman uses the term 'precarious manhood' to refer to the ways that hegemonic masculine ideals 'exis[t] in a precarious state and needs to continuously be reaffirmed through social proof and validation' (Vandello et al., 2008, p. 1327). The precarity of masculine ideals – including those associated with the 'good soldier' and 'good military' – results in a perpetual need for service members and institutional leaders to act in ways that validate, reinforce, and prove their capacity to live up to these ideals.

1.4 Good Soldiers Are Allowed to Be Bad According to Military Exceptionalism

The concept of military exceptionalism captures the complex and sometimes paradoxical ways that 'good militaries' and 'good soldiers' are seen to be both disciplined protectors of the nation – exercising legitimate violence – *and* untamable as always capable of indiscipline and illegitimate violence. Through my analysis, I show how ideals about military institutions and culture presume *both* romantic notions of camaraderie, band of brother loyalty, hierarchy, honourable masculinity *and* regular – often accepted – dysfunctional practices such as hazing and war crimes. Similarly, the 'good soldier' has been historically constructed *both* as a stoic, professional, and controlled man that follows orders *and* as an untamed warrior that occasionally – but understandably – 'comes undone,' either as a result of being overcome by witnessing violence and the spectre of 'evil' in war zones (S. H. Razack, 2004), or from the burden of his role as defender of the nation.

This approach to understanding military exceptionalism, institutionalism, and soldier identity makes space for two alternative approaches to understanding and researching MSV. First, it allows for considering how sexual violence might be read not simply as rogue 'bad apple' soldier behaviours but as an articulation of masculine power – a method of putting women and feminized others 'in their place' – and an expression of impunity and supremacy. Second, it creates an opportunity to explore justifications of MSV, and the stories we tell about MSV as efforts to reinforce the ideal of the 'good' military and soldier. As Black feminists remind us, the use of legitimate and illegitimate forms of violence has been a strategy for demonstrating settler colonial power throughout history. More specifically, the ability to construct social rules and break them with impunity has been a privilege often only available to white men. There is a clear role for 'good militaries' and 'good soldiers' in narratives that depict some nations as 'civilized' and responsible for maintaining order in 'dark' and chaotic places around the world (S. H. Razack, 2004). 'Good militaries' are depicted as exceptional institutions bearing the burden of protecting society against internal and external 'dark' threats, with 'good soldiers'– who are often white males in the public imaginary – leading these efforts and exerting their power and masculinity through their self-control and commitment to service.

For both the 'good' military institution and the 'good' soldier, the subjects they must focus their attention on – 'uncivilized' communities, the 'dark' enemy within, and fragile women – become the foil to their honourable efforts. Peacekeepers 'lose it' and commit violence or 'descen[d] into madness' when confronted with 'savagery' (Razack, 2004, p. 10); senior officers cannot contain their 'primal urges' and commit assault when working in close confines with women; and entire units commit war crimes in Afghanistan because of a combination of 'frustration' and 'boredom' (Boal, 2011). In each of these scenarios, the 'savages', 'civilians', or 'women' are to blame for pushing the noble and disciplined soldier and institution to the brink and forcing them to commit illegitimate acts. The 'good military' and 'good soldier' are models of white civilized power. Meanwhile, 'dark threats' and weak women encumber and interrupt this power, resulting in an 'understandable' and legitimate loss of control. The dysfunctional behaviours that result from such loss of control are rarely read by society as a sign of weakness; rather, they are seen as a symbol of the burden of white masculine protection.

Military exceptionalism operates in service of maintaining the military as a legitimate and powerful institution and the 'good soldier' as a legitimate and powerful figure in the nation. The concept of military exceptionalism is often leveraged to smooth out and erase what would otherwise seem to be glaring contradictions in military institutions and soldier behaviour. Through military exceptionalism, stories of crime and dysfunction can be reframed to instead centre the soldier and their institutional burden as dedication. Through military exceptionalism, war crimes can be framed as expressions of soldier exhaustion and frustration, illegal hazing activities can be cast as necessary for bonding and 'soldiers blowing off steam' to prepare and relieve them of the weight of service. Military exceptionalism can also help explain how sexual assault accusations can be described as efforts to ruin the reputation of the military and destroy 'good' men's careers. Notions of military exceptionalism make space for casting any evidence of military dysfunction as a biproduct of institutional and soldier dedication and commitment. In turn, militaries can retain their status as revered institutions, defined by order, discipline, and honour, even in the face of seemingly contradictory evidence – such as instances of war crimes, high MSV rates, or hazing practices – through this concept of military exceptionalism.

Military exceptionalism therefore signals more than the unique nature of the military, or the idea that militaries must be held to separate standards; instead, it signals a deeply held and taken-for-granted conviction that service member and illicit institutional activities are evidence of the burdens of protecting the nation, not dysfunction. Military exceptionalism also legitimizes institutional and soldier dysfunction and powers narratives that gaslight victims of MSV. In the following section, I explore this concept of institutional gaslighting in greater depth.

1.5 Institutional Gaslighting

While the exact genealogy of the term 'gaslighting' is contested, many associated it with the 1938 play 'Gas Light', which depicted a husband cruelly and slowly working to convince his wife she is losing her mental capacity, including by gradually dimming the lights and denying to her that it is getting darker. Gaslighting has typically been described as a phenomenon within intimate relationships, whereby the 'gaslighter' takes advantage or abuses trust. The term 'gaslighting' has become increasingly popular in the past decade. Feminists in particular have used it to describe the frequent ways that women and marginalized groups are made to second-guess their position, question their feelings or sanity, and are described as overly emotional or reactive (Lalonde, 2020; Kennedy-Cuomo, 2019). Gaslighting is widely described as a gendered phenomenon in which feminized subjects are made to question their positions by those with more power, typically men. Paige Sweet argues that, 'gender inequality is a condition of possibility for gaslighting,' and identifies gaslighting as a key feature of a patriarchal system that treats women as feminized subjects as inexpert, overly emotional, and irrational (Sweet, 2019). Although there are variations in how gaslighting is defined and described, it effectively captures having one's sense of reality questioned or diminished, and being made to doubt one's experience or sanity by those in positions of power.

Black feminists have argued that gaslighting as a popularized term has been undertheorized and used simply as shorthand to describe making women 'feel crazy' or disempowered. Such depictions often centre white women and their male partners, ignoring the multiple forms of oppression that might lead to an individual's experience of being made to feel irrelevant, irrational, and unable to reliably narrate their own experience. Elena Ruiz, for example, argues that this typical rendering of gaslighting '[i]s a settler conceptual ruse that diverts critical attention away from structural epistemic oppressions that continue to underwrite the colonial project' (Ruíz, 2020, p. 690). Ruiz argues that rather than just undermining women, or making them feel 'crazy,' gaslighting is an 'enduring process' aimed at sustaining existing power structures, including 'the maintenance, upkeep, and regeneration of white supremacy' (Ruíz, 2020, p. 694). Thus, gaslighting should be seen as a response to efforts to resist existing power structures.

Black feminists have developed the term 'structural gaslighting' to describe the systemic efforts to sustain existing power structures by denying or obscuring the 'patterns of harm they produce and license' (Berenstain, 2020, p. 733). Racial gaslighting is described as a form of structural gaslighting that involves a range of activities that may include denying racism or undermining or rendering irrelevant the lived experiences of those that experience racism (Ruíz, 2020; Berenstain, 2020).

While structural gaslighting refers to broad efforts to maintain patriarchal and white supremacist systems, institutional gaslighting refers to the roles that institutions play in this process of reinforcing and sustaining existing power structures, including denying and obscuring the harmful and oppressive effects of these structures. Institutional gaslighting includes political strategies to resist critiques of the institution or discredit evidence that undermines the authority or carefully crafted image of the institution. Kennedy-Cuomo argues that institutions – particularly trusted institutions like universities and militaries – use a range of tactics to respond to any evidence that undermines their image, including distracting, trivializing, and denying (Kennedy-Cuomo, 2019). Writing on institutional responses to sexual violence, she concludes, '[W]hen someone expects to trust the judgement of an institution, but the institution then betrays justice, survivors are gaslighted' (Kennedy-Cuomo, 2019).

Gildersleeve et al.'s research on Black and Brown students' experiences illustrates how institutional gaslighting operates and its impact. They found that Black and Brown doctoral students 'questioned their sanity' due to the ways their experiences were denied or sidelined even as universities made claims to take 'diversity' seriously. In this example, the university institution does not gaslight racialized students by denying the existence of racism; rather, the institution uses an adjacent set of discourse that acknowledges the significance of 'diversity,' yet constructs an understanding and set of policies to address diversity and inclusion that completely sideline Black and Brown students and their experiences. Students are made to feel 'gaslit' because they operate in an institution that claims to support and be an ally, yet ultimately operates in ways that continue to marginalize them. Berenstain's work highlights how structural gaslighting is often perpetrated by people or institutions that position themselves as 'well intentioned' and 'allies' (Berenstain, 2020).

Drawing from this work, I argue that institutional gaslighting should be recognized as a strategy that includes narratives and counter-narratives, that work to legitimize existing practices and power structures and discredit or undermine any efforts to resist these structures. Paige Sweet describes gaslighting as a gendered political strategy that 'amplifies power' by 'manipulating other's sense of reality' and associating others with 'feminized unreasonableness' (Sweet, 2019, p. 871). I argue that the power of institutional gaslighting is not in denying one's reality; rather that it involves institutions acknowledging aspects of an oppressive phenomenon like racism and sexism while it simultaneously renders the lived experience of those impacted by this phenomenon irrelevant. Institutional gaslighting includes having your experience of a phenomenon explained to you by those in power in ways that are not simply inadequate but diminishing, and in ways that ultimately legitimize existing structures and present any problems as having been 'solved.' In sum, institutional gaslighting is not only about denying that a social phenomenon exists, but rather about creating narratives about that phenomenon that render entire communities and their experiences irrelevant and disregarded.

As a result, institutional gaslighting involves institutions constructing partial and limited accounts of structural forms of oppression and presenting them to those that are impacted by these phenomena. Gaslighting occurs when individuals are made to feel like it is their problem if their experience does not align with the existing institutional account of their own experiences. Institutional gaslighting, therefore, can involve sexual assault policies and 'equity and diversity' statements that are constructed and enacted in total isolation from those who understand and experience sexism and racism. It can also be used to capture the pattern of those in power explaining social phenomena like sexism, sexual violence, and discrimination to women, who often have a privileged knowledge of these issues because of their own experience. Feminists have used the term 'mansplaining', for example, to describe the experience of men explaining phenomena to them that they have existing expertise on, or experience of (Solnit, 2014).

Conceptualized in this way, the concept of institutional gaslighting becomes useful for analysing MSV rhetoric. In this project, I am not simply identifying MSV rhetoric and narratives to show that factual inaccuracies exist; rather, I use the concept of institutional gaslighting to explore how MSV rhetoric may reinforce existing power dynamics and deny or erase experiences that could challenge carefully crafted images of the good military and good soldiers. Again, my analysis does not pit institutional accounts against survivor accounts of MSV. As indicated in the introduction, my analysis is centred on rhetoric and public media coverage of MSV not as it compares to victim stories, but as a tool for understanding the patterns and potential myths that exist in these public conversations.

In my analysis, I explore several ways that MSV rhetoric might operate as a form of institutional gaslighting. First, I explain how MSV rhetoric and ideas of military exceptionalism might feminize those outside of the military and render them 'inexpert' and incapable of generating legitimate critiques, questions, or analysis of military institutions or practice. Second, I note how MSV narratives and rhetoric can convey the message that the problem of MSV is 'solved' or in the process of being solved. This gaslights victims, because it implies that their story or response is not illustrative of a systemic problem, but an example of isolated incidents that they are already addressing. Third, I explore how rhetoric may acknowledge the problem of MSV, but also present solutions to the problem that almost totally exclude victims' experiences, thus creating a sense that the institution is the authority 'handling' the issue, even as it denies the experience of victims. In this sense, the analysis explores how civilians who question military authority as well as sexual violence victims who seek justice can both be gaslit through MSV rhetoric. Public media coverage of MSV was a logical site to explore the public conversations of MSV and to consider how military exceptionalism and institutional gaslighting may be implicated in these narratives.

1.6 How and Why Do You Read 3,000 Articles About Sexual Violence?

The central aim of this book is to explore public discourse about military sexual violence, with particular attention paid to the narratives and rhetoric found in these public conversations. As indicated in the introduction, I draw heavily from the work of Sherene Razack (2004) who argues that case study analysis and attention to the construction and articulation of national mythologies is illustrative of how power, sexism, and racism operate within a society. In her work on Canadian soldier atrocities in Somalia, Razack reminds us that 'the hold that mythologies have should not be underestimated. They have the power to make a nation replace tortured and dead bodies with traumatized soldiers. Mythologies help the nation to forget its bloody past and present.' (Razack, 2004, p. 9). Razak notes that work that draws out national myths and narratives is not only critical, but also potentially transformative; identifying national myths and rhetoric makes it possible to dismantle and move beyond these narratives to create space for alternative ways of envisioning and organizing society.

To understand national narratives and myths about MSV, I analysed 30 years of media coverage in three different countries. The remainder of this chapter is organized around the following key questions that help explain the rationale and specifics of my approach to this research: What are rape myths and MSV rhetoric? Why conduct a media analysis, and what does it mean to analyse narratives in media? And how do you manage – both logistically and emotionally – an analysis of hundreds of articles from three different countries?

1.7 What Are Rape Myths and MSV Rhetoric?

Historically, rape has been treated – legally and socially – as a distinct and severe form of sexual violence. As conversations about sexual violence have evolved, there is an increased call to move away from categorizing and creating a hierarchy of forms of sexual violence. Instead, advocates promote a survivor-centered approach to understanding sexual violence, which sees different forms of violence on a continuum rather than in a hierarchy. This approach privileges the experience and needs of survivors, without presuming a correlation between forms of assault and extent of impact. As a result of these shifts in discourse about sexual violence, the terms 'rape culture' and 'rape myths' do not just pertain to the crime of rape; rather, they are often used broadly to refer to a range of forms of sexual violence, broader cultures of sexual violence, and deep and embedded myths about all forms of sexual violence.

But what exactly does the phrase 'rape myth' mean and how is it useful in analysing MSV? Janice Du Mont and Deborah Parnis describe rape myths as 'prejudicial, stereotyped, or false beliefs about rape, rape victims, and rapists' (Du Mont, J. and Parnis, D, 1999, p. 304). In her book, Helen Benedict identifies common rape myths, including versions of 'she was asking for it,' 'perpetrators are villainized and unknown "others",' 'women regularly lie about rape,' 'good guys don't rape,' and 'men have an uncontrollable sexual drive that can lead to rape' (Benedict, 1992). Each of these myths serves to remove accountability for rape from perpetrators and distracts attention away from any systematic acknowledgement of, or accounting for, sexism or rape culture.

Sabine Sielke (2002) distinguishes between data, or purported 'facts' about sexual violence, and discourses about sexual violence and rape. She argues that representations of rape are always partial interpretations that are shaped by – and also reproduce – norms about sex, gender and power. Drawing on Frederic James, Sielke argues that narratives about rape 'reflect a fundamental dimension about our collective thinking and our collective fantasies about history and reality' (2002, p. 2). This approach aligns with a broader literature that views rape as a 'cultural practice' (Wieskamp, 2018, p. 138). It treats narratives about rape as deeply political and reflective of cultural norms and values. It is also in line with Black feminist arguments that structural violence is never accidental, but always perpetrated to sustain a wide and interconnected set of power structures (Ruíz, 2020; bell hooks, 2000).

Sielke introduces the idea of 'rhetoric of rape' to refer to patterns in public conversations about rape. The term 'rhetoric' here is used to refer to familiar ways of framing a subject that are persuasive and may even come to be understood as common sense. Sielke argues that public discussions of rape are dominated by consistent narratives and myths that constitute a 'rhetoric of rape' (2002). Analysing this rhetoric and the patterns of narratives and myths associated with rape provide important insights into how power operates in a society. As

Sielke argues, 'transposed into a discourse, rape turns into a rhetorical device, an insistent figure for other social, political and economic concerns and conflicts' (2002, p. 2). Similarly, Helen Benedict argues that media coverage and representations of sex crimes are politically significant because 'sex crimes have a unique ability to touch upon the public's deep-seated beliefs about gender roles' (Benedict, 1992, p. 3). In turn, examining dominant narratives can reveal a great deal about not only the phenomenon of sexual violence but also social attitudes about sex, gender, and power.

Researchers who have examined rape myths in the civilian context found that several consistent myths are regularly reproduced in media coverage and public conversations about sexual assault, with significant social and political implications (Sampert, 2010; Easteal, Holland and Judd, 2015). As mentioned earlier, the findings include that acceptance of rape myths is associated with increased negative perceptions of rape survivors, (Lonsway and Fitzgerald, 1994) lower conviction rates and shorter sentences for perpetrators, (Finch and Munro, 2004) and police reports that reproduce rape myths (Shaw et al., 2017). Existing work on rape myths and rhetoric is important but has often centred on gender and power dynamics while ignoring race and militarism.

While I find the concept of 'rape myths' useful, my analysis centres on narratives (or complete stories) told about MSV. Existing work on rape myths has highlighted important and problematic tropes and myths; however, my analysis is designed to identify complete narratives and stories told about MSV rather than simply untruths, or misperceptions about MSV.

Before providing details on the stages of analysis, I also want to clarify how I use the concepts of 'frame' and 'narrative' in this book. Essentially, I treat framing and frames as the process and outcome of selecting what elements or aspect of an issue to focus on when writing (Scheufele and Tewksbury, 2006). Frames can incorporate both subtle and overt choices used to create meaning out of a broader topic and often form a 'central organising idea or story line' (Scheufele and Tewksbury, 2006, p. 12). Frames can also promote '*a particular problem definition, causal interpretation*, moral evaluation, and/or treatment recommendation' (Entman, 1993, 52 emphases altered). In my analysis, I selected a single frame for each article by considering both the focus of the article as well as what was presented as the source of, or solution to the problem of MSV.

I use the concept of narrative to refer to complete, consistent, and familiar stories told to make sense of a phenomenon (Shepherd, 2012; Razack, 2004). I treat narratives as stabilizing forces; they are the through-line that emerges across multiple articulations of a problem or issue (Stavrakakis, 2007, p. 42). I especially draw from Sherene Razack's approach to narrative, defined as 'the ways that stories are assembled for public consumption' (Razack, 2004, p. 18). Razack argues that when it comes to national militaries, public narratives often erase or decenter individuals impacted or implicated in the story and focus instead on the perspectives of those in power. For Razack, narrative analysis is always attuned to deconstructing narratives, or 'looking for the way in which they are about something else' and 'the process of separating the experiences of individuals from the way their stories are assembled for our consumption' (Razack, 2004, p. 18).

1.8 Why Focus on Media Coverage?

Military sexual violence is an issue that impacts individuals deeply; focusing on media coverage and public conversations, rather than victim stories and testimonies, may seem counter to the feminist commitments of this book. While a media analysis is certainly not the only way to approach this topic, I argue that there are three main benefits to such an approach.

First, examining media coverage of MSV allows for a direct comparison between media coverage of MSV and civilian sexual violence, which means it is possible to determine whether there are rhetorics, narratives, and gendered myths unique to media coverage of MSV. As indicated in the introduction, existing work on civilian sexual assault has found that 'rape myths' – or commonly-held but false stereotypes about rape and rapists – persist in media coverage (Sampert, 2010). Existing work also demonstrates that media coverage often privileges a masculine perspective and diminishes or ignores women's interests or experience (Marzolf, 1993; Rhode, 1995; Sendén, Lindholm and Sikström, 2014; Wadham and Bridges, 2020). Women are also routinely portrayed as men's property, frail victims, or uninformed and apolitical subjects in media coverage on civilian sexual violence (Rhode, 1995; Sampert, 2010; Alexopoulos and Siefkes-Andrew, 2018). Despite this important research on media coverage of civilian sexual violence, there is little scholarship that explores the possible commonalities or distinctions between how media covers sexual violence between civilian and military contexts (for exceptions see Bell, Stein and Hurley, 2017; Alexopoulos and Siefkes-Andrew, 2018; Kasinsky, 1998; Andrews, Connor and Wadham, 2019). The few studies that do focus on media coverage of MSV find that it relied on gendered tropes, blamed victims, and included 'little serious journalistic reporting from a feminist perspective' (Wadham and Bridges, 2020, p. 15; Kasinsky, 1998).

The systematic analysis of media coverage provided in this book extends existing work on civilian sexual violence by considering the stories we tell about MSV and whether there are consistent gendered tropes and 'rape myths' particular to media coverage of MSV. Media analysis is useful because it provides a means for systematically identifying prominent narratives, or stories that are told about MSV. Existing scholarship has pointed out that how we make sense of social phenomena – like MSV – is often bound up in particular narratives and myths. These organizing stories capture widely held ideas about why MSV occurs, as well as if (and how) it can be alleviated. Existing feminist work on narrative and dominant public myths indicates that such stories often reflect and reproduce assumptions about women's places in society (Brownstone et al., 2018). Although media coverage is not the sole source of material that can be used to access these stories and narratives, media representations are a useful place to begin to understand and make tangible the patterns, stories, and overarching myths associated with MSV in the hopes of ultimately unravelling them.

A second reason media analysis is useful is because the media provides one of the few sources of information about military activities. There is a military-civilian divide where most civilians only come to know about military issues and problems through media coverage (Bell, Stein and Hurley, 2017; Kasinsky, 1998; Wadham and Bridges, 2020). Therefore, the way that the media frames and conveys information about military phenomena, including MSV, is politically significant (see also Crosbie, 2011). In their analysis of media coverage of military scandals, Andrews et al. (2020, p. 271) argue that military organizations manage public attention and scrutiny strategically to 'maximiz[e] the benefits of eliciting positive public attention while minimizing the consequences that can arise from negative public attention'. They argue that strategies for managing public attention include routines and techniques that are worthy of study and attention. In her analysis of media coverage of 'Tailhook,' which refers to a 1991 Navy and Marine Symposium that resulted in over 80 allegations of sexual assault (and is explained in greater detail in the next chapter), Kassinsky found that 90% of news stories published between 1991 and 1995 relied on official government sources, with few independent sources and almost no investigative reporting on the Tailhook case (Kasinsky, 1998). As the media landscape continues to change and resources became more limited, it is likely that the media may rely increasingly on official military or government sources; they are, therefore, an important source for understanding institutional strategies to 'minimize consequences' and respond to MSV.

A third value of media analysis stems from evidence that media attention can produce tangible results in terms of public knowledge and political responses. Thomas Crosbie and Jensen Sass' 2017 analysis of media coverage of MSV identifies patterns in media coverage and political responses to MSV and concluded that increased coverage led to more scrutiny and political accountability and commitment to the issue (Crosbie and Sass, 2016). In short, media coverage is both political and has political implications, in terms of encouraging a political response to an issue. As I show in the analysis that follows, there is almost a 'call and response' relationship between the media and military institutions whereby high-profile cases generate public declarations by military or government leaders of 'renewed commitments' or 'zero tolerance.' A systematic analysis of media coverage provides an opportunity to better identify this relationship between the media and the institutions, and to identify the significance of media coverage in evoking a political reaction.

1.9 Managing an Analysis of Hundreds of Articles on MSV

1.9.1 Logistics

There were a number of logistical considerations for managing and analysing media coverage of MSV between 1989 and 2017 in Australia, Canada, and the United States. First, I selected top print media outlets in each country, not only to keep a consistent subject of analysis (given that the selection period precedes digital publication and social media), but also because print media usually take on a 'primary agenda-setting [and framing] role' (Thakker and Durrant, 2006). For each case country, I selected newspapers based on circulation as well as regional representation. The specific newspapers for each country were:

United States: USA Today, Wall Street Journal, New York Times, LA Times

Canada: *Globe and Mail, Toronto Star, Vancouver Sun, Winnipeg Free Press*

Australia: *Courier Mail, The Age, Sydney Morning Herald, Daily Telegraph*

The time period was set from 1989 to 2017, an almost 30-year span, to allow for the longitudinal comparison of reporting patterns. In searching articles, I used the following terms for all cases: 'armed force' or 'armed forces' or 'defence force' or 'defence forces', as well as 'sexual' (to triangulate any articles using terms such as 'sexual assault', 'sexual violence', 'sexual harassment'). For the US I also added the terms 'Marines', 'Air Force', 'Navy', 'Army', 'Coast Guard', and for Canada I included the term 'Canadian Forces'. I limited articles to those discussing only intra-service sexual crimes. Initially, these search terms resulted in a vast number of articles, many of which were not relevant to the analysis, including articles focused on consensual fraternization, the sexual preference or sexual orientation of service members, extra-service sexual violence (violence perpetrated by service members against civilians), and other types of sex-based discrimination such as discrimination against pregnant women. After excluding thousands of articles on this basis, 1,487 remained within the analysis, made up of 297 Canadian articles, 214 Australian articles, and 976 US articles.

The first stage of analysis focused on identifying the number and variety of potential frames across the coverage. As indicated earlier, I define 'frame' as the central organizing idea of an article. The goal of the framing analysis was to identify the core focus of a media article as well as what was presented as the source of, or solution to the problem of MSV. Frames were determined through an iterative process. First, two researchers read a sample of 20 articles and made suggestions for an initial set of frames. Then, the same researchers coded another 20 articles, selecting one frame for each article, to refine the frames until no new categories emerged. In total, seven frames were identified, which were found reliable in that they appeared to work both across time as well as across case countries. After establishing the frames, two researchers coded all the articles independently to one another, to establish inter-coder reliability; a third researcher was brought in to settle any cases where coding differed, which happened for less than 5 per cent of articles. Articles that did not seem to have a strong or clear organizing idea were categorized as having 'no frame.'

The second stage comprised a narrative analysis aimed at identifying coherent narratives, rhetorical tools, and potential myths told across the media coverage. While the framing analysis was used to determine the number and variety of potential frames, as well as the frequency of key terms across the coverage, the narrative analysis identified overarching stories and dominant gendered myths within the coverage. Laura Shepherd has long called for scholars to identify the 'stories we tell' within discourse. Shepherd argues that 'our cognitive frameworks are (re)produced in and through the stories we tell ourselves and others' (Shepherd, 2012, p. 3). In addition to identifying coherent stories told about MSV, the analysis is focused on identifying myths and potential gendered or rape myths associated with MSV. Drawing from my own previous work, attention to myth is not focused on identifying truths or false stories. Rather, the goal is to 'trac[e] the origins of these ideas in order to destabilize them and to create space for their critique and unraveling' (MacKenzie, 2015, p. 13).

1.9.2 Emotions

Sexual violence is personal and living in a patriarchal society means that most people – particularly women – have a deep, extensive, and intimate knowledge of sexual violence through personal experience, the witnessing of violence, and offering of support to survivors of violence. There seems to be a growing consensus that individuals can be impacted, or triggered, by conversations, media coverage, or other forms of content they consume. Feminists have also considered the emotional impact of research on the researcher and the need for scholars to not only situate themselves, but also be transparent about the ways their personal experience shapes their research process and the way the research, in turn, impacts them (Reay, 1996; Hordge-Freeman, 2018; Davis and Khonach, 2019).

With all this in mind, it is difficult to fully capture the methodological and personal strategies that my research team and I used to manage this research. In short, this work is hard. Reading thousands of articles on sexual violence was not only triggering at times, but was also variously deflating, infuriating, and numbing. I cannot recount the myriad of ways this work impacted me personally, nor can I speak for the researchers I collaborated with and hired to work with me on this project. Instead, I want to focus this section on some of the specific strategies we developed – some successful, and some not – to manage the emotional impact of this work.

After initiating this project in 2016, I realized that one of the challenges of reading large swaths of media coverage came from the solitude and inability to discuss ideas and talk through aspects of the coverage. I hired two researchers to work with me to help code the Australian media content as a 'proof of concept' for the methods that I would come to use for the rest of the book. Having a team not only helped ensure inter-coder reliability when it came to selecting frames, but it also gave us a chance to talk through the material and its impact on us. During this stage, the two other researchers and I met regularly to check our coding and discuss any significant or outlying cases. These chats were also an opportunity to support one another and share our reactions to cases or patterns.

Based on this experience of having a small team analyse the Australian content, in 2019 I established a 'pop up' research lab, designed to further develop methods for analysing MSV media content, while at the same time offering training and mentoring for students and Early Career Researchers (ECRs) in how to conduct a media analysis. The lab was set up to include methods development and analysis of media content with a team of ten researchers and experts working in a shared office space over the course of three weeks. The team included media experts, journalists, leading scholars working on sexual violence or media analysis, and ECRs. One of the goals of the lab was to create a supportive space where researchers could conduct an analysis of media coverage of sexual violence, have set breaks to discuss challenges or issues that arise, and have regular exchanges to ensure inter-coder reliability. I held meetings each morning with the team to set the agenda, and the lab was catered so that we had the chance to debrief over our meals. Pairs of researchers analysed the same sets of articles and, at the end of each day, discussed whether their coding and analysis was consistent and flagged any disagreement. In cases where coding differed, a third coder could be brought in from the team to discuss and settle the difference.

There were benefits and drawbacks to the pop-up lab design. The lab was a success in that the majority of the media material was coded for frames and ECRs received training, experience, and mentorship. Additionally, while doing this research in a team setting certainly does not fully alleviate the emotional and logistical challenges, I think it helped. The setting gave us a chance to debrief, share problems and coping strategies, and to find solidarity and levity in the face of challenges brought up by some of some of the material. It also allowed us to work on a rotating schedule to help avoid research fatigue.

However, there were also times when the 'togetherness' worked against the goals of the lab and it was clear that researchers – including myself – needed more space and time alone to think, process the material, and simply work quietly. Most scholars are used to long periods of solitude so three weeks of 'togetherness' sometimes felt overwhelming. Although the lab involved a team of researchers, the subsequent analysis and writing was still a solitary – and somewhat lonely – project. My previous experience with conducting work on difficult subjects (including sexual violence in war) means that I have a range of personal strategies for managing the mental toll that this work can take; however, these strategies have their limits and there inevitably remains an emotional burden to navigate.

1.10 What Are the Limits of a Media Analysis?

A media analysis cannot tell us everything about rape myths and national narratives about MSV, and there are several limitations to the methods I have chosen for this book. I acknowledge that the media landscape is changing rapidly, and an analysis of traditional print media excludes a range of non-print outlets. Nonetheless, the media outlets I selected remain among the highest circulated nationally and, given the time frames needed to identify patterns in narratives, established media sources were the most appropriate choice.

I also acknowledge that a media analysis does not centre the voices and perspectives of victims; however, as I clarify in the introduction, this book is about *public* narratives and myths of MSV, making media content an appropriate source of focus. Finally, media coverage is only one source of what inevitably converges into public conversations about MSV. Military press releases, government and military leader statements, public inquiries or press conferences, and court cases, are among the other sources that contribute to public knowledge of, and narratives of, MSV. Again, I argue that media coverage is the main source of information from which most people get their information about MSV; more people will read the news than a press release, court document, or research report (though media outlets often draw from military press releases or comments made by political leaders). It is impossible to draw a clear line between media framing and military and government public relations; however, my goal is to understand public narratives, not to provide a media critique or analysis. Thus, I am interested in analysing any material made available to the public through the media and do not try to distinguish official statements from opinion pieces or other types of journalism.

This chapter has clarified and elaborated on the theoretical concepts and methods that shape the analysis that follows. While there are always benefits and limitations associated with the decisions of how to study a particular problem or issue, I am confident that a media analysis of nearly 30 years of media coverage of MSV across the three cases results in rich and unprecedented material that allows for unique insights into patterns in media coverage, trends over time, and overarching narratives. Returning to Razack's work on myth, identifying these patterns, trends, and narratives facilitates both critique and efforts to dismantle: first, it provides unique insights into national gendered tropes, myths, and deeply held beliefs about the military; and, second, it informs efforts to unravel these patterns and transform public conversations about MSV.

2 | *Defining Scandals*

2.1 Introduction

Before moving to an analysis of media coverage of MSV and the stories told about MSV in each of the case study countries, it is necessary to provide three sources of background and context. This chapter outlines definitions, data, and defining scandals related to military sexual violence (MSV) in each of the case study countries. This provides important context for the remainder of the book and supports one of the secondary arguments of the book: that what we know about MSV is political, limited, and largely shaped by scandal, or high-profile incidents that garner significant media attention.

This chapter, and the book more broadly, does not focus in depth on MSV statistics and data. In fact, while some data is included, one of the goals of this chapter is to illustrate that MSV 'data' is not a more objective, clear, or accurate source of information about MSV compared to media analysis and story-telling about MSV. Rather, I argue that MSV statistics and data *are* stories told by institutions; they are shaped by which information is collected and made available, and which information is erased, ignored, or kept private. A second key argument put forward in this chapter is that certain types of incidents of MSV drive media coverage and policy responses to the issue. Media attention ebbs and flows dramatically, and often centres on cases that are considered particularly salacious or extraordinary. These high-profile cases, or scandals, often set the tone for conversations decades to come and may even come to be so well-known that a short-hand moniker or phrase is used to signal the event, such as 'Tailhook.' Given that this book centres on media coverage and public conversations, it is essential to have a sense of these key defining scandals.

The following section provides an overview how MSV is, and has been defined in the United States, Canada, and Australia. This is followed by an overview of available data on MSV, and the politics and limitations of data collection. In the final section, graphs of media coverage are provided, highlighting peak points linked to high-profile cases, or MSV defining scandals. This is followed by a brief description of each of these defining scandals.

2.2 Definition

It is important to understand how military sexual violence (MSV) is defined in each of the case study countries. There is no commonly accepted, or universally-agreed upon definition of MSV, which makes it challenging to compare data or discuss the issue beyond national contexts. The types of terms that militaries use in reference to sexual violence are constantly changing, yet often remain distinct from the terminology used to describe civilian sexual violence. Adding further confusion, researchers use a variety of terms and focus on different aspects of assault or harassment when collecting data or conducting research on MSV. As already indicated, I use the term MSV because it captures the range of sexual assault and violence activities. By contrast, Sadler et al. 2018 use sexual assault in the military (SAIM). Wood and Toppelberg (2017) use the term 'military sexual assault' (MSA) to refer to assaults where the victim and perpetrator are servicemembers. The range of terms used by institutions and external researchers can lead to confusion and data that is not comparable or possible to analyse over time. Firestone and Harris (2009) explain: 'empirical measures of sexual harassment have been as disparate as the definition, leading to diverse findings and ambiguous conclusions.' Firestone and Harris (2009) also note that sexual harassment and assault have often been considered a 'women's problem', meaning that there is less research focused on men's experiences (p. 88). In all three case study countries for this book, separate data on male victims of MSV has not been consistently collected or published, making it difficult to understand the scope of the problem and reiterating stereotypes that only women are victims. The remainder of this section provides a summary of the definitions used by each of the case countries in relation to MSV.

The Canadian Armed Forces (CAF) and Australian Defence Forces (ADF) both use the term 'sexual misconduct' and include sexual misconduct as a sub-category of 'unacceptable behaviours' (a term used regularly by the ADF) or 'improper conduct' (the term regularly used by CAF). Similarly, both the CAF and ADF refer to a 'spectrum' of behaviours, or as the CAF puts it in their definitions, 'the range of attitudes, beliefs, and actions that contribute to a toxic work environment' in their definitions (National Defence, 2022). The ADF defines sexual misconduct as including, but not limited to 'sexual discrimination; sexual harassment; sexual offences; and the recording, photographing or transmitting of incidents of a sexual nature without the knowledge and consent of all parties' (Australian Human Rights Commission, 2012). The CAF defines sexual misconduct as 'conduct of a sexual nature that can cause or causes harm to others' and includes a listing of activities that constitution sexual misconduct, from jokes to forms violence (Government of Canada, 2021).

The term sexual misconduct is a problematic and political term. It reflects the history of treating sexual assault and harassment as simply one of many forms of misconduct. In fact, neither Australia nor Canada's Defence Forces collected regular and disaggregated data on sexual misconduct until 2008 (Australia); and in 2015 (Canada) instead, incidents of sexual misconduct were simply included in general data on all forms of misconduct. The term sexual misconduct is also distinct from civilian legal terms, such as sexual assault, sexual harassment, and sexual violence, which centres victims and frames the incident in terms of the experience of the act for victims rather than merely as a violation of a military code of conduct.

The US Department of Defence did not recognize sexual assault as a distinct offence until 1992 and only developed an official policy regarding sexual assault in 2004, with the creation of the Sexual Assault Prevention and Response Office (SAPRO). The US military separates sexual assault from sexual harassment, with the main distinguishing factor seeming to be physical contact and/or the use of force. Sexual assault is defined in Article 120 of the Uniform Code of Military Justice (UCMJ) as: ' ...intentional sexual contact, characterized by use of force, threats, intimidation, abuse of authority, or when the victim does not or cannot consent. Sexual assault includes rape, forcible sodomy (oral or anal sex), and other unwanted sexual contact that is aggravated, abusive, or wrongful (to include unwanted and inappropriate sexual contact), or attempts to commit these offenses' (U.S. Navy's Military Sealift Command, 2022). Sexual harassment is defined as 'unwelcome sexual advances, requests, or other sexualized behaviour pervasive enough to create a hostile working environment or involving the threat/ promise of employment-related punishments/

rewards.' Researchers and activists have criticized this distinction between harassment and assault, noting that 'both have similar effects on victims' (Thomsen et al., 2017, p. 366).

Thomsen et al. point out that the Department of Veterans Affairs (VA) does not make a distinction between assault and harassment, using the term military sexual trauma (MST) to refer to the range of forms of sexual violence (Thomsen et al., 2017). Although the Department of Defence does not explicitly use the term, military sexual trauma (MST) is a term used by the Department of Veterans Affairs (VA), the federal government, and also by researchers. The VA defines MST as sexual assault or repeated or threatening sexual harassment during military service. Under US Federal Law MST is defined as 'psychological trauma, which in the judgment of a VA mental health professional, resulted from a physical assault of a sexual nature, battery of a sexual nature, or sexual harassment which occurred while the veteran was serving on active duty, active duty for training, or inactive duty training' (The National Resource Center on Domestic Violence, 2022). MST is often framed as correlated with, or a variant of, post-traumatic stress (PTS) or post-traumatic stress disorder (PTSD) (Kimerling et al., 2010; Street et al., 2008), which is generally perceived as a condition that impacts men exposed to combat trauma. Within the military context, sexual trauma has been shown to pose at least as great a risk for PTSD as combat experience (Kimerling et al., 2010, p. 330).

2.3 Data

In this section, I focus on the politics of data collection and highlight how defence forces have failed to collect and publicize consistent and reliable data related to MSV. Methods of data collection in each country is staggeringly inadequate, inconsistent, haphazard, and defy basic principles of data collection. I argue that a brief glimpse of the history of data collection related to MSV signals a lack of commitment and possibly even a concerted effort to obscure the extent of the problem. It is impossible to know the intent behind data collection practices in the case study countries; however, it is possible to conclude that, up until the past few years the Canadian, Australian and US militaries did not have enough information to even understand the scope of the problem of MSV, let alone address it. The following section presents available data on MSV in each of the case study countries, and explores the politics of data collection, including the limits to existing mechanisms of reporting. I preface this discussion by noting that, in addition to the limits to available sources of data, there is also evidence of a culture of underreporting, particularly among women. Research suggests that only 15 per cent of victims of MSV report the incident (DART, 2016, p. 31; Australian Human Rights Commission, 2012); therefore, all incident and survey data discussed below should be read with the understanding that these are likely the tip of the iceberg in terms of total number of victims.

2.3.1 Canadian Data

The 2016 Survey on Sexual Misconduct in the Canadian Armed Forces (SSMCAF) found 27 per cent of women in the armed forces had been sexually assaulted in their careers, and members of CAF were twice as likely to be sexually assaulted compared to the general population. It was also found that female regular force members are four times more likely than males to report and were more likely to identify their supervisor or other higher-ranking personnel as the perpetrator. Another survey was released in 2018, with similar findings; a notable difference was that 30 per cent of regular force members reported fearing negative consequences of reporting MSV. The 2016 survey was initiated after former Supreme Court Justice Marie Deshamps conducted an external review of this issue and is scheduled to be conducted every two years. Prior to the 2016 survey, one of the only sources of data on MSV came from a Statistics Canada survey on Canadian community health. This survey was not intended to measure MSV in the forces but does include references and some statistics as part of the larger survey of mental health in the CAF. Unfortunately, this information is not currently publicly available. There is not much data on MSV at military colleges, with the exception of a 2019 Statistics Canada survey and report.

In Canada, the media have been an important source of MSV data and media reporting has highlighted the gaps in data on this issue. News articles going back to the 1990s contain a variety of personal stories, estimates of numbers of sexual assaults, and data from freedom of information requests. The series of investigative articles published by Maclean's Magazine (starting in 1998) provide important insight into the prevalence of MSV prior to any formal collection of data.

2.3.2 Australian Data

In 2021, it was reported that sexual assault complaints within the ADF had risen to an eight year high (Stayner, 2022). In 2020/2021 187 cases were reported compared to 160 in 2019/2020. There is limited access to two methods of measurement of MSV in Australia: surveys and incident reports. Prior to the sexual harassment scandal on the HMAS Swan in 1992, and the Senate inquiry that followed, 'the ADF had compiled no records on the incidence of sexual harassment in the Services' (Australian Parliament, 1994, p. 297). In response to a request made by the Standing Committee to disclose the incidence of sexual harassment and violence, the ADF manually combed through all its reports – police, incident, personnel, or unit – and found 137 and 121 reported cases of sexual harassment and abuse respectively between 1989 and 1993 (Australian Parliament, 1994, p. 298). Given that these incidents were reported to several outlets that did not systematically collect the data – including the Defence Force Ombudsman and the Sex Discrimination Commissioner – it is unlikely that these numbers reflect all, or even the majority of incidents (Australian Parliament, 1994, p. 296–9). Incident report statistics were not published again until 2012, in response to the 'Skype sex scandal' which is described later in this chapter.

Surveys are another method used to gather information about the incidence of sexual harassment and misconduct in the ADF. The first survey into sexual misconduct in the military was conducted in 1987 by Major Kathryn Quinn. Her study was conducted with about one-fifth of the female servicewomen serving at the time (1,400 respondents), who were asked across twelve items if they had ever been exposed to a sexist environment (53 per cent reporting yes); received direct comments or inappropriate contact (42 per cent reported yes); or received attempts at sexual coercion from a superior (11 per cent reported yes). In 1995, this survey was conducted again (3,100 respondents), but with key differences: the survey was issued to both men and women, identified five areas of misconduct (gender harassment, offensive sex-related behaviours, unwanted seductive behaviour, sexual bribery or threat, and sexual imposition), and asked only about incidents in the preceding 12 months. Due to the changes made to the survey, the data cannot be compared to earlier surveys, making it impossible to measure trends in harassment or assault rates. Also, the language of the 1995 survey was both vague and unique; it is unclear why terms like 'unwanted seductive behaviour' or 'sexual imposition' were used in place of harassment, assault, or misconduct. Despite the unique nature of the survey, it is worth noting that the results indicate 62 per cent of women and 7 per cent of men experienced gender harassment (again, a term used to capture offensive sexual behaviour, seductive behaviour, sexual bribery/threat and sexual imposition). In the breakdown of results, data also indicates that 76 per cent of women and 60 per cent of men experienced offensive stories, jokes or posters.

The ADF also has the Unacceptable Behaviour Survey, a survey first administered as part of the 'Grey Review' in 1998, which was a comprehensive review of ADFA's policies and practices to deal with sexual harassment and sexual offences. The survey was conducted annually between the years 2000 and 2009 in the ADF, but the majority of its results are not available to the public. In 2000, the Unacceptable Behaviour Survey attracted 1,320 female and 1,040 male respondents and asked about harassing behaviours experienced or witnessed in the past twelve months. Results showed that 73.3 per cent of female and 63.6 per cent of male respondents had experienced harassing behaviours. In 2013, the survey attracted 1,536 female and 4,756 male respondents. It found that 55 per cent of female respondents and 37 per cent of male respondents experienced harassing behaviours (AHRC 2014, p. 42, n. 78). It appears that the surveys were discarded around 2011, after being described in a Defence Brief as unreliable for being 'inconclusive and possibly inflated' (Pearce, McKean and Rumble, 2012, p. 120). As a result, the survey does not appear to have been conducted again until after the outbreak of the 'Skype sex scandal'.

In 2012 the AHRC also conducted a survey with 1,000 service people (500 men and 500 women), asking about their experience of sexual harassment (based on the legal definition) in the past five years. Results showed that 25.8 per cent of women and 10.5 per cent of men said they had experienced harassment. Some of this data is available, but not comparative to earlier surveys because – as with other surveys – the population surveyed changed from year to year and key questions were changed in different versions of the survey.

2.3.3 US Data

The US has garnered significant negative attention when it comes to MSV, in part because of the persistent high rates, high profile cases, and popular media attention, including the 2012 documentary *The Invisible War*, which garnered an Oscar nomination. Although the US military has and continues to exhibit serious limitations in the ways MSV is addressed, when it comes to data collection, it should be seen as an international model. As indicated, Canada and Australia collect incident and survey data across the services and typically publish this information every two years. This information does not provide a breakdown of where the incidents are occurring, which rank or service the victims and alleged perpetrators are, or the outcomes of cases. There is also no regular data collected on military colleges or service academies. As a result, it's almost impossible to map patterns in MSV in these two countries, which would allow for the development of more targeted measures to address it. Part of this may be that, unlike the strong Congressional oversight and vocal political advocates for addressing this issue – like Senator Kirsten Gillibrand – in the United States, there are simply no political champions of this issue in Canada or Australia.

While historically, the US military was equally as poor at collecting data on MSV, in recent years this has changed. The result is that the amount and range of data on MSV in the US is almost overwhelming. The US Department of Defence releases an Annual Report on Sexual Assault in the Military. The two main components of this report are incident reports and survey data. The survey data comes from the Workplace and Gender Relations Survey of Active Duty Members (WGRA), which was revised substantially in 2014. This survey is anonymous and allows service members to provide information about sexual assault experiences and perceptions that may not have been formally reported. This allows for the US military to observe the 'gap' between the number of official incident reports and the percentage of service members who anonymously report experiencing sexual assault. This is important information since there is ample research indicating a 'culture of underreporting' and multiple obstacles or reasons why service members may not report. Incident and survey data helps us to understand the extent to which MSV is underreported and may also provide insights into why victims are hesitant to report.

The range of data collected in the Annual Report is incredible. It includes detailed data on victims and alleged perpetrators, including rank, gender, age, and service; data on which reports were restricted or unrestricted and how many, if any, restricted reports become converted within the year; and a breakdown of incidents in terms of rape, aggravated sexual assault and sexual assault, abusive sexual contact, wrongful sexual contact, indecent assault, forcible sodomy, and attempts to commit offences. In addition to data on victims and perpetrators, the report provides information about command actions taken in response to sexual offences, any transfer requests related to offences, data on reports of sexual assault in Combat Areas of Interest (CAI), or deployments that involve active operations, and a breakdown of which countries these incidents were reported. Finally, there is data on allegations and perceptions of retaliation among victims of sexual assault.

Another major report with important information on MSV in the United States is the Annual Report on Sexual Harassment and Violence in the Services Academies. This report includes detailed information on incidents and trends at the US's service academies. Other major source of data on MSV in the United States comes from media reporting, and academic and institutional research. Media reports and investigations can explore specific aspects of the issue and may include data obtained by investigative reporting or freedom of information requests. For example, the Associated Press collected data indicating that sexual misconduct was the reason why at least 30 per cent of military commanders were relieved from command since 2005. RAND has published a number of research reports on MSV that are independent and thoroughly researched (Matthews et al., 2021). There is much more detailed research on MSV in the US and this research often focusses on specific aspects of the issue, including rates and experiences in particular services and the long-term impacts of MSV on service members. For example, in their research on the US Air Force, Bostock Daley (2007) found that 28 per cent of active-duty Air Force members had been victims of forceable rape at some point in their lives, with military perpetrators accounting for 30 per cent of the most recent rapes. More than a third (38 pr cent) of the active-duty women reported experiencing at least one or more sexually harassing behaviours from a boss or supervisor while in the military (Bostock and Daley, 2007, p. 936). Daley also found that 69 pr cent to 97 per cent of victims of sexual harassment did not see the behaviour as sexual harassment (Bostock and Daley, 2007, p. 937). This type of focused and in-depth research reveals various facets to the problem of MSV. In this case, the research indicates that women in military might have higher life experience of sexual violence prior to service and that they may be less likely to define and rationalize their experience as assault.

Since 2014, the US has collected excellent and comprehensive data on MSV; however, there remain some gaps in this data. One such gap relates to the Special Forces. The budget and mandate of the Special Forces has grown exponentially over the past two decades. Special Forces members are donated by their respective services and there are indications that SOF leaves it to respective branches to collect data on MSV. This means there may be a data gap in terms of MSV rates within SOF units, which are renowned for having a particularly hyper masculine and exclusive culture. The following section outlines the 'defining cases' or high profile cases of MSV in each country.

2.4 Defining Cases

One of the unifying factors of all three case study countries is that high-profile MSV events- sometimes referred to as 'scandals' – have come to shape public conversations and even policy responses related to this issue. The following section is not a comprehensive history of all high-profile cases of MSV in the three case study countries; nor does it offer a definitive account of what constitutes 'scandal' or high-profile. Rather, it provides a summary of what I have identified as 'defining cases'. I identify cases as defining when they garner a significant and prolonged amount of media coverage. I used graphs of the total number of media articles focused on MSV over time in each case country to illustrate the ways that coverage culminates around several of these defining cases. As indicated earlier, some defining events are so ubiquitous that they go on to be referred to with a commonly understood name, such as 'Tailhook', and 'the Skype sex scandal'. Given how important these cases have been in garnering public attention and provoking internal reviews or policy changes, it is necessary to briefly map out these cases. They have been designated as defining cases because of significant media coverage, but also due to the lasting impact most of these events had on the ways that MSV was discussed. In each section below, I begin with a visual graph of total number of media articles, with each defining case identified with a letter. This is followed by a description of these events and, in some cases, an indication of the policy implications or flow on effects of these cases.

2.5 USA Defining Scandals

United States

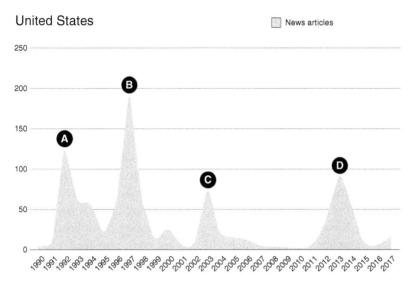

Figure 2.1 USA Defining Scandals.

2.5.1 (A) Tailhook 1991

The first peak in media coverage on the graph in Figure 2.1 (A) signals media coverage related to a 1991 US Navy and Marine Corps aviation officers Symposium, in which approximately 83 women and 7 men were sexually assaulted by male military officers (Winerip, 2013). It became infamously referred to simply as 'Tailhook.' Tailhook might be better understood as a global defining case given how the events associated with the event gained international media coverage and sparked global conversations about sexual violence in the workplace and sexual assault and harassment in armed forces. Offences linked to the symposium ranged from sexual assaults to physical assault, public intoxication, nudity, and harassment at the Las Vegas Hilton. Officers were reported to have wandered around the hotel wearing t-shirts that read 'women are property' and to have participated in sexual activities such as the 'gauntlet' (Lancaster, 1993). The official Pentagon report detailed 'activities as: "butt-biting"; "belly/navel shots" (drinking tequila from the navel of a willing partner); "leg shaving" (squadrons held contests inviting women to let male aviators shave their legs and pubic areas); "zapping" (slapping squadron stickers on breasts and buttocks); and "ballwalking" (exposing one's testicles) (Lancaster, 1993).

Media attention to the offences occurring at Tailhook heightened in 1992 when Paula Coughlin, a Navy lieutenant who attended Tailhook, came forward alleging that she had been sexually assaulted while at the conference. While the Navy initially handled the investigation, complaints that the investigation was ineffective resulted in the Department of Defense taking over the inquiry. The Pentagon report on the conference described the Navy's Tailhook sexual assault scandal as 'the culmination of a long-term failure of leadership' and recommended disciplinary action against at least 140 Navy and Marine officers (Lancaster, 1993). Those named in the investigation ranged from civilian contractors to high-ranking officials such as the Chief of Naval Operations. While no officers were disciplined for the sexual assaults, approximately 40 officers were punished for 'conduct unbecoming an officer' or for making false statements and several high-ranking military officials were removed from their positions (Lancaster, 1993).

The scandal itself led to unprecedented scrutiny of the US Military's attitude towards women in the forces and came to be seen as 'a watershed event that ... brought about cultural change' (Lancaster, 1993). The military was criticized in the media and by the public, which resulted in several new policies. These include the April 1993 announcement by Secretary of Defense Les Aspin that going forward women would be allowed to compete for assignments in combat aircraft, additional Navy ships for women as well as a proposal to Congress to remove barriers in assigning women to combat vessels. While the military widely stressed that they were adopting a zero-tolerance reform, most initiatives that came out of Tailhook focused on allowing women to serve in more combat roles as opposed to addressing or preventing rampant sexual abuses and providing support for survivors.

2.5.2 (B) Aberdeen Proving Grounds 1996

In 1996 several allegations of assault were raised against male members of the Ordnance Center and Schools' military faculty, primarily drill sergeants. The victims were largely young female training students. The events occurring at Aberdeen Proving Grounds in 1996 were widely viewed as the Army's very own Tailhook. Perpetrators were accused of engaging in an abusive ring called 'Playing the Game or GAM – game a la military' (Shadley, 2016), which was a contest whereby men compared how many recruits they could have sex with. Unlike Tailhook, the events at Aberdeen resulted in 12 men facing charges, of which 3 supervisors were eventually convicted and given prison time – two for rape and one for adultery. Instructors at Aberdeen were accused of behaviours ranging from sexual harassment to rape and sodomy and the resulting investigations revealed a clear pattern of systemic abuses of female trainees.

The events at Aberdeen also called into question issues of consent in the context of power dynamics such as student, teacher relationships. While sexual contact between students and instructors had been banned in the Army prior to the events occurring at Aberdeen, the scandal refocused attention on the phenomena, as many of the instructors implicated in the scandal claimed that while inappropriate, the encounters were consensual. Several of the officers on trial even attempted to use claims of consent in their defence. For example, at the time of the trials, the Baltimore Sun published an article interviewing the family and friends of accused Capt Derrick Robertson describing him as good man who had been led astray in a consensual relationship with a trainee. Robinson, who pled guilty to adultery, sodomy, and other offenses, was described as 'so clean; so straight' by a former teacher (Erlandson, 1996). Thus, the issue of fraternization came to the forefront much more than it had in Tailhook.

Another unique aspect of the Aberdeen scandal was the fact that all of the 12 men facing court-martial were identified as Black while all of the victims in the scandal were white. Therefore, Aberdeen is also unique for its positionality in broader issues of race and racism in the US Military. At the time, several prominent Black leaders and members of Congress suggested that Black men involved in the Aberdeen scandal were being unfairly targeted and attempted to bring attention to larger issues of racial discrimination in the US Military alongside the sexual assault scandal (Courtl and Milloy, 1997).

The Aberdeen scandal resulted in the aforementioned prison time for three men, multiple demotions, early retirements, and other discharges for the men involved. It also resulted in the Army creating a hotline for survivors, which led to the discovery that 'GAM' was common at many other training facilities and several other men faced discipline or prison time as a direct result of investigations resulting from the hotline. Further, like Tailhook, the scandal contributed to a public perception of the military 'as a cauldron of sexual misconduct and hostility toward women' (Titunik, 2000, p. 230).

2.5.3 (C) Air Force Academy 2003

In early 2003 the Air Force began investigating at least 56 reports of sexual assault or rape stemming back a decade at the Air Force Academy in Colorado. The cases included both service member and civilian victims. Victims coming forward reported a number of tactics used by the institution to deter reports of sexual assault, including being faced with counter charges of lesser infractions of academy rules and recommendations for expulsion from the Academy. Female cadets also reported that they were warned about a 'culture of rape' that they were expected to accept or risk being 'hounded from the academy' (New York Times, 2003). News coverage included attention to the fact that between 1996 and 2003 99 reports of sexual assault were received by the academy's hotline, but no cadet had been court-martialed for allegedly sexually assaulting another cadet during this period (Fiore and Kelly, 2003).

2.5.4 (D) Lackland 2011

Fifteen years after the Aberdeen series of assaults and charges, a similar scandal came to light at Lackland Air Force Base where it was revealed that trainees were alleging sexual assault at the hands of their trainers. The offences occurred in 2009 both during and after basic training at the Texas base. Like in Aberdeen, offences ranged from fraternization to rape. Uniquely, the scandal was brought to light not only by the complaints of trainees but also by the reports of other instructors. By the end of the investigation, the Air Force had identified 43 female victims.

In this scandal 17 male instructors were implicated and 35 instructors were removed from duty pending investigations. Two lieutenant colonels also lost command of their units as a direct result of the scandal. Several of the accused instructors accepted plea deals and gave evidence against other Military Training Instructors (MTIs) as part of the terms of the agreement. The longest sentence given out was to the first man accused, Staff Sgt. Luis Walker of the 326th Training Squadron who was brought up on 28 charges which included rape, aggravated sexual contact, and aggravated sexual assault (New York Times, 2012). During his trial, he gave evidence against other MTIs, and 10 trainees gave evidence against him. He was convicted of all 28 charges, required to register as a sex offender and sentenced to 20 years in prison. Walker killed himself in prison in 2014 after serving two years. Other MTIs were given sentences involving prison time, hard labour, and demotions in rank and pay.

Like Aberdeen and Tailhook, the Lackland Basic Training scandal resulted in increased media attention and public scrutiny regarding MSV and the safety of junior female service members. As was the case in the other two scandals, military officials attempted to portray the Lackland scandal as an outlier; officials pointed to the fact that many of the instructors came from the same unit as evidence that it was a localized not systemic problem (Lawrence, 2012). Officials also highlighted the issue of fraternization and 'consensual' relationships as opposed to rape and downplayed the scandal's place in a larger history of sexual scandals. The scandal led to the military looking into the numbers of female MTIs in the forces. At the time, only 11 per cent of MTIs were women and officials considered that hiring more women as MTIs or having only women MTIs supervise female trainees could be viable solutions to the problem (Lawrence, 2012).

2.6 The Invisible War 2012

In 2012, *The Invisible War* documentary was released to critical and popular acclaim. The documentary drew on interviews with veterans from the Armed Forces who recounted their assaults. The film also showcases home footage from the veterans of their lives after being assaulted and the ongoing effects of military sexual trauma. Alongside these interviews, the filmmakers interviewed advocates, journalists, and active and retired military officials. The film highlights many of the issues that were brought to light by scandals such as Tailhook and Aberdeen, which are referenced many times in the film. Reviewers found that the film 'suggests that one in five serving female officers has been sexually assaulted' – the male victim rate is unclear – and that women know that making a complaint will entail a humiliating and futile procedure in which the original experience will be made a thousand times worse: the complainant will always be disbelieved and can be subject to a Saudi-type counteraccusation of 'adultery' (Bradshaw, 2014).

The film personalized the issue and made it widely accessible to the general public, which resulted in both the military and the US government engaging in several different reforms. Most notably, a number of the survivors who appeared in the film filed lawsuits against the Forces. For example, survivor Kori Cioca (and others from the film) filed *Cioca v. Rumsfeld* which alleged that Donald Rumsfeld and Robert Gates 'failed to prevent sexual assaults within the military forum and failed to properly punish those individuals guilty of committing these offenses' (Mesok, 2016, p. 54). The lawsuit was later dismissed on the grounds that personnel cannot sue the forces for injuries that occurred while they were in service. The New York Times claims that the film directly resulted in more women coming forward with their own experiences (Risen, 2013a).

The film also inspired military leaders and government officials to implement reforms and legislation focused at combatting the epidemic of MSV in the forces. On 16 April 2012, at the time, Secretary of Defense Leon Panetta issued a directive ordering all sexual assault cases to be handled by officers at the rank of colonel or higher as opposed to the prior practice of allowing commanders to handle cases within their own units (in his 2014 memoir, Panetta directly named the film as the inspiration for this directive) (Daniel, 2012). Similarly, Senator Kirsten Gillibrand highlighted the film as being hugely influential on her work to create legislation aimed at reducing MSV. However, the most notable impact may be the National Defense Authorization Act for Fiscal Year 2013, signed by then President Barack Obama, which formed special victims units that specifically investigated MSV, and introduced policies that attempted to limit retaliation against survivors and prevented people with felony sex abuse convictions from enlisting (Bennett, 2013). The military also used the film in training materials and screened it for many branches of the Forces.

2.7 High Profile Cases Post-2017

While this book focuses on media coverage between 1989 and 2017, it is helpful to note high profile cases that have occurred outside this period. This helps signal the ongoing cycle of scandal, commitment to change, and silence surrounding this issue in all three case study countries. In the US context, this includes another series of allegations that instructors were harassing female recruits at Fort Benning in 2017. This case is particularly noteworthy because in 2017 Fort Benning had only recently started allowing women into its training programs for combat positions, with the first integrated class of infantry recruits graduating in May 2017 (Fortin, 2017). There is very little public information available about the 2017 incidents, as the names of victims and perpetrators were not released by the Forces. One source suggested that around five male instructors were suspended and under investigation (Kube and Connor, 2013).

It was not revealed what the consequences were for the men involved in the scandal, however, the commander of one of two battalions was relieved of his duties shortly after the media began reporting on the scandal (Kube and Connor, 2013). Officials refused to confirm whether the commander being released was related to the incidents but it was acknowledged that he lost his command due to 'loss of confidence in his ability to command' (Meyers, 2017).

Media attention related to the scandal drew parallels to similar cases such as Tailhook, Aberdeen, and Lackland, especially the latter two due to the continued attention given to the unequal power relationships between trainees and instructors. Officials were much more vocal in this case in condemning the systemic nature of MSV. For example, Sen Kirsten Gillibrand was quoted as saying 'the Fort Benning investigation shows that the Pentagon hasn't lived up to its promises to crack down on sexual assault' (Kube and Connor, 2013).

2.8 Vanessa Guillén 2020

A second recent high-profile case involved the murder of Vanessa Guillén, a 20-year-old US Army soldier, at the hands of fellow soldier Aaron David Robinson on 22 April 2020. Guillén's dismembered and burned body was not found until 30 June. Her killer was located through his civilian girlfriend Cecily Anne Aguilar who was also charged with evidence tampering after the body was discovered. Aaron David Robinson committed suicide after escaping custody in Fort Hood. The case against Aguilar is currently being prosecuted.

Prior to her disappearance, Guillén disclosed to her family that she was experiencing sexual harassment at the hands of a sergeant at Fort Hood. She claimed that the complaints of other women against the sergeant were dismissed and that she felt she needed to handle the issue herself as opposed to making an official report. Guillén also revealed that she was afraid for her mother's safety when her mother wanted to make a report for her (Brito, 2020). Shortly afterwards, Guillén disappeared and the CID and FBI were brought in to investigate. In the aftermath of the discovery of her body, criticisms against the military were brought forward by Guillén's family, the public, the media, and government officials. Guillén's mother blamed the military for her daughter's death and was outspoken in her belief that the military killed Robinson as part of a widespread cover up (Guillen, 2021). As a result of Guillén's death, an investigative report surrounding her death as well as the events following it was undertaken by the military.

The report found that the Army made multiple mistakes which led to Robinson escaping custody at Fort Hood. Furthermore, it found that 'Specialist Guillén had been sexually harassed, but not by the soldier who the Army believes killed her, and that the suspected killer had also been accused of unrelated sexual harassment' (Phillips, 2021). Furthermore, the report revealed that Guillén had in fact approached her chain of command regarding two incidents of sexual harassment by a superior officer (propositioning her for sex and approaching her in the shower) but both complaints were ignored and not pursued. Following the release of the report, 21 soldiers and officials involved with the case were punished. In December of the same year, an investigation into the overall culture of Fort Hood was also conducted and found that a large number of soldiers had died there as a result of suicide or homicide. Furthermore, it was found that there were 'major flaws' that left women 'vulnerable and preyed upon, but fearful to report and be ostracized and re-victimized' (Phillips, 2021).

As this case occurred in the wake of the #MeToo movement in Hollywood, there was an outpouring of anger and protest surrounding the circumstances of her death. Soldiers began sharing their experiences of MSV under the hashtag #IAmVanessaGuillen. Legislation was introduced in Guillén's name that would make sexual harassment a crime in the military while another bill was introduced that would place the responsibility for investigating MSV under independent military lawyers (Phillips, 2021).

2.9 Canada's Defining Scandals

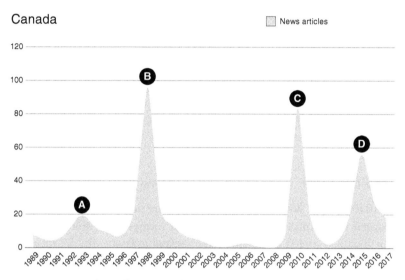

Figure 2.2 Canada Defining Scandals.

2.9.1 (A) Department of Defence Internal Survey and Human Rights Complaints

The small increase in media attention to MSV in Canada in 1993 shown in Figure 2.2 (A) was the result of data published from a 1992 Department of Defence internal survey, which reported that a quarter of female service women experienced sexual harassment at work. It is important to remember that this period was when the CAF was also facing the Somalia inquiry[1] so some articles linked the issue of sexual harassment to broader issues of discrimination – particularly racism and evidence of white supremacy within the CAF. In 1993 media attention also centred on the annual report of the Canadian Human Rights Commission, which found that 13 of the 128 complaints related to sexual harassment brought to the commission were from the military – the highest number of any federal institution.

---

[1] In 1993 news broke of Canadian soldiers torturing and killing Somali children and teenagers while on a humanitarian mission in Somalia. The acts were documented by photographs and further details of the incidents came out following a public inquiry. The torture and abuse became popularly referred to as the 'Somalia affair' and 'Somalia inquiry', with the inquiry revealing broader forms of systemic abuse and sexism in the CAF.

2.9.2 (B) 1998: Maclean's magazine feature article

In 1998 Maclean's magazine published an expose on MSV in the Canadian Forces that featured the stories of several survivors; it garnered significant national and international attention. Maclean's then published three follow-up cover stories highlighting the systemic nature of MSV in the CAF. It is important to note that this came several years after the infamous 'Tailhook' case in the US, which was largely seen to have uncovered the significance of the problem of MSV in the US and initiated a trend in centring the voices of victims of MSV.

2.9.3 (C) 2010: Colonel Russell Williams scandal

In 2010 Russel Williams, a previous commander at CFB Trenton, is charged with murdering two 38-year-old women, two home invasions that included forced confinement and sexual assaults, and 82 incidents of break and enter. The story draws intense media coverage because of the brutal nature of the murders, the number of victims, and the details of the perpetrator's underwear fetish. This case also highlighted issues of power abuse between commanders and lower-ranking service members and showed limitations to a system of reporting and justice that would allow for a perpetrator to commit so many crimes before being arrested.

2.9.4 (D) Ongoing series of events

There were a series of events between 2013–2015 that sparked increased media attention to MSV. The first was the publication of results from the 2013 Canadian Forces Mental Health Survey, that sought to measure rates of post-traumatic stress disorder (PTSD) and sexual assault experiences. At the time, CAF used the term 'military work-related sexual assault' (MWSA) and found that 14.8 per cent of service members experience unwanted touching, 7.6 per cent experienced force sexual activity, and 15.5 per cent experienced sexual assault in a workplace related setting. Over 90 per cent of all of these recorded instances were committed by another CAF member or DND employee.

In 2014 MacLean's and L'actualité co-published another high-profile expose entitled 'Our military's disgrace.' The article centred on Stéphanie Raymond, who accused a former Warrant Officer André Gagnon of assaulting her. Raymond was dismissed soon after she filed the complaint with Military Police in 2012. After repeated appeals Gagnon was charged and the CAF Chief of Staff issued an apology and admitted the CAF had failed in their handling of the case. In addition to featuring Raymond's case, MacLean's/L'actualité featured the stories of dozens of victims of MSV and the results of extensive research into data and processes related to MSV in the CAF. Partly in response to the attention generated by the features, the CAF called for an external review led by former Supreme Court Justice Marie Deschamps.

In 2015 former Justice Marie Deschamps was tasked with conducting an external review of policies, procedures, and programs in relation to sexual harassment and assault. After interviews and focus groups that included over 700 participants, Justice Deschamps issued her external review, which became widely referred to as 'the Deschamps Report'. The report found an 'underlying sexualized culture in CAF that is hostile to women, LGBTQ members.' It also found that as members moved up the ranks, they became desensitized to this culture. The report also found that the current policies and claims of 'zero tolerance' were insufficient, that the CAF had not adequately defined, collected data on, or understood the nature of the problem of MSV. The Deschamps report included 10 key recommendations, the foremost of which was to establish an independent body that would handle MSV complaints, data collection, justice, and victim support.

Following the publication of the Deschamps report, the CAF issued 'Operation HONOUR,' which was a series of policies and strategies designed to change the culture in the Forces and stop inappropriate sexual behaviours. It was launched by then Chief of Defence Staff Jonathan Vance, who later faced multiple allegations of MSV. Operation HONOUR used militarized language and metaphors to describe a 'mission' to eliminate sexual misconduct. After the 2015 launch, there was an increase in reports of sexually inappropriate behaviour (40 reports in 2015, 300 reports in 2017). An internal report (2018) described this increase as evidence that service members trust the system; however, internal data also indicated service members did not trust the system and 30 per cent feared negative reprisal for reporting MSV.

As part of Operation HONOUR, the Statistics Canada Survey on Sexual Misconduct in the Canadian Armed Forces was initiated in 2016. As indicated earlier, the survey found 27 per cent of women in the armed forces had been sexually assaulted in their careers, and members of CAF were twice as likely to be sexually assaulted compared to general population. It was also found that female regular Force members were four times more likely than males to report and were more likely to identify their supervisor or other higher-ranking personnel as the perpetrator. Another survey was released in 2018, with similar findings; a notable difference was that 30 per cent of Regular Force members reported fearing negative consequences of reporting MSV.

In 2017 the Globe & Mail released findings of 20 months' worth of investigations into MSV in the CAF. The report included one of the clearest insights into the scope of the problem; it presented data from 870 police forces, provided detailed insights into the military justice process, and highlighted key inadequacies of the system identified by victims of MSV. As a result of the report, 179 cases of sexual misconduct were reviewed, and 23 cases were re-opened.

2.10 Australia Defining Scandals

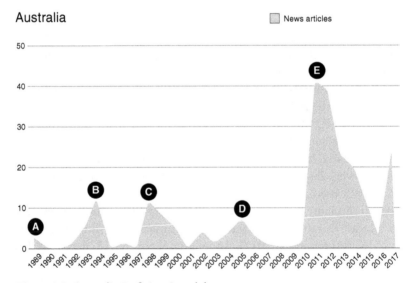

Figure 2.3 Australia Defining Scandals.

2.10.1 (A) 1989 Inquiry into the Royal Australian Air Force (RAAF)

The first small increase in media coverage in the Figure 2.3 (A) relates to an inquiry that took place into RAAF behaviour at the Edinburgh base north of Adelaide. The investigation was initiated after a

29-year-old airman was charged with raping a 19-year-old woman. Over 400 women who had trained at the base in the two years prior to the incident were interviewed by RAAF investigators. The investigations brought to light allegations against several RAAF staff and highlighted a toxic culture that included regular fraternization between female recruits and male superiors as well as hazing and initiation rituals that were sexualized and abusive.

2.10.2 (B) 1992/1993 HMAS *Swan*

The increase in media attention in 1992 and 1993 centred around coverage of systemic sexual harassment and abuse allegations on the HMAS Swan Navy vessel. The federal government announced a Senate inquiry into incidents on board the vessel during a 1992 deployment. A former navy Lieutenant and doctor, Dr. Carole Wheat claimed that she was raped on board the ship. There was a flurry of media coverage when news broke that another female Seaman Wendy Flannery asked a British soldier to intentionally break her leg so she could escape sexual harassment on board the HMAS Swan. Flannery recounted to media outlets that she and another female language specialist on the Swan developed a plan that would allow them to leave the ship due to injury because the environment of harassment was constant and had eroded their mental health. Allegations of widespread sexual harassment and assault emerged and Dr. Wheat claimed that she had been told of multiple rapes at navy bases (Daly, 1994a). The Senate inquiry revealed more assaults on women and a culture of gender discrimination and harassment on the ship. The man accused of Dr. Wheat's rape was acquitted by court-martial and while the inquiry found that all accusers had been harassed, the subsequent Senate inquiry discredited many of the women's claims and reversed a censure against the captain.

2.10.3 (C) 1998 Australian Defence Academy Review and RAAF 'sex romp'

In 1998 a six-month inquiry into sexual misconduct at the Duntroon Australian Defence force Academy (ADFA) found an embedded culture of sexism and binge drinking (New York Times, 2003). The report concluded that cadets were subjected to pressure and humiliation and that the ADFA's leadership model had a strong bias towards physicality and masculinity, with leaders emphasizing 'loyalty to your mates' above 'doing the right thing'. It was also noted that cadets also equated power with authority, and third-year cadets frequently abused this power. The same year this report was released, three RAAF officer-trainees faced a court-martial over what was called a 'sex romp' at the Point Cook air base (Green, 1998). The Point Cook case involved an alleged 'wild party' that included naked dancing and alleged simulated sexual acts.

2.10.4 (D) 2005 Ongoing rampant sexual misconduct

There was no single incident in 2005 that sparked increased media attention; however, a common thread to the headlines this year was that sexual misconduct was *still* rampant. Data was released indicating that complaints of misconduct had actually increased across the services, highlighting not only a lack of improvement in addressing sexual misconduct, but a worsening of the problem. Many of the articles discussed evidence that the sexualized and toxic culture identified several years earlier remained, despite frequent claims of 'zero tolerance' by military leaders.

2.10.5 (E) 2011 'the Skype sex scandal' and fall out

What came to be known simply as the 'Skype sex scandal' in 2011 attracted far more media attention than any previous case of sexual misconduct in Australia. The case involved Air Force academy cadet 'Kate' and a fellow cadet, Daniel McDonald. McDonald broadcast consensual sex with 'Kate,' without her knowledge or consent, to six fellow male academy members in another dorm room. Still photos of the video were then circulated among cadets via mobile phones. Frustrated with the institutional response, Kate went to the media, and a major news broadcaster broke the story. A day after the story broke, Kate was called in by the Air Force for an unrelated disciplinary hearing. Then Minister of Defence was openly critical of the ADF's handling of the incident and announced six concurrent defence reviews, including two by the Sex Discrimination Commissioner, Elizabeth Broderick, (one into treatment of women at the academy and one more broadly into promotional pathways for women in Defence); the Andrew Kirkham, QC, review into the way the academy handled the Skype incident; a 'cultural stocktake' of binge drinking, use of social media and personal conduct in military establishments; a review of the management of complaints by the ministry; and a review by a law firm of allegations of abuse stretching back six decades to receive allegations of other abuse (this review found about 700 new allegations deemed credible). Kate was eventually discharged from the military on psychological and medical grounds, and reported to have lost her career, and suffered poor health and an interruption to her education as a result of the incident. Daniel McDonald and Dylan Deblaquiere were both charged with sending offensive material over the internet without consent and McDonald was also charged with an act of indecency against Kate. Despite the charges, both received 12 month good-behaviour bonds, with the Judge concluding that they did not deserve jail time for the incident. McDonald was subsequently briefly suspended from the academy for allegedly founding a group requiring members to perform homosexual acts on each other, called 'Love of my Life'.

The wave of reviews that were initiated following the Skype sex scandal shed new light on the nature of the problem of misconduct in the ADF. The Defence Abuse Response Taskforce (DART) ran for four years and received 2,439 complaints. The DLA Piper report also exposed that the findings of a 1998 investigation never led to any trials for 24 people accused of raping fellow cadets. Broderick's first report found that more than 70 per cent of female academy cadets had been sexually harassed.

Just as media attention to the Skype scandal was waning, a new story broke of soldiers engulfed in what came to be called the 'Jedi Council' sex scandal. The Jedi Council involved allegations that up to 17 men, including officers and combat veterans, used the military email system to exchange pornographic material, including explicit images of several women taken without their consent. As a result of the investigations, six service members were removed from the ADF, with the alleged ringleader sentenced to 15 months of community service for telecoms offences.

2.11 The Cycle of Scandal, Action, and Inaction

Analysis of nearly 30 years of MSV media coverage reveals a distinct pattern of scandal- attention-policy response – silence – in which high-profile cases lead to a dramatic increase in media attention, a series of proposed reforms or commitments by military or political leaders, followed by an almost total drop off in attention – sometimes for a decade. While it is understandable that media outlets would cover stories of MSV that are unique and would be of interest to the public, 30 years of media coverage reveals that a handful of cases have garnered the majority of total news coverage of MSV. In doing so, these cases come to shape the public imagination about the problem of MSV. This scandal pattern also highlights how policy responses to MSV seem to be driven primarily by public attention, rather than ongoing political commitments to solving the issue. Finally, the scandal pattern also demonstrates that in the absence of high-profile cases, public attention and political efforts to address this problem diminish almost entirely. This is important to note because in the same period of time that media attention ebbs and flows dramatically, MSV rates in each country remain relatively consistent, and in some cases increase. As a result, it seems that political commitments are more connected and responsive to media coverage than to data or evidence about MSV rates. Again, this reiterates the importance of media coverage in shaping not only public conversations about MSV, but in initiating and sparking policy responses to address the issue.

2.12 Conclusion

One of the main purposes of this chapter is to make the case that data about MSV is not an objective or clear-cut way to understand the problem. The ways that the problem of MSV is defined and measured is political, limited, and varies over time within and across the case study countries. In short, what we think that we objectively know about MSV are stories shaped by decisions about how to name the problem, how to measure and map it, and which information to keep private or make publicly available. A second goal of the chapter was to highlight how a small number of cases in each country garnered the majority of attention to MSV and subsequently shaped debates and discussions about MSV. These high profile cases are important to understand not only because they garner significant media coverage but also because there is clear evidence that the cases, and the media attention they provoke, inspires political responses, including in the form of calls for reviews, or suggestions of policy reform.

3 | *The US Band of Bros*

This chapter maps out nearly 30 years of media coverage of MSV in the US and identifies the frames and consistent stories and overarching narratives found through this analysis. Before presenting the findings of this work, it is important to outline several ways US military and media coverage of MSV in the US is broadly unique – and specifically distinct from Canada and Australia. Having lived in each of the case study countries and studied their militaries for years, I have a strong sense of the relationship between national culture, national identity, and military culture. I think this knowledge helps in my analysis of media coverage and in picking up on distinctions and cultural idiosyncrasies. I have studied the US military for over a decade, including visiting a number of military posts, interviewing service members, and presenting my work on the military to various US civilian and military audiences. What is perhaps most unique about the US military is how Hollywood ideals and representations of the institution become enmeshed with national and international perceptions of it and its status as a global cultural reference point.

In short, the US military is a pop culture icon. Hollywood movies, tropes, and tag lines associated with the US military have international recognition and form the context for public understandings of the institution and media coverage of MSV. For example, as I argue in my 2015 book, the band of brothers myth signals a deeply held and widely-recognized story of the unique bonds all-male units have, which are necessary for fighting war. Other tropes and phrases like, such as 'no man left behind,' 'the few, the proud,' are specific to the US military, yet broadly recognized due to their reproduction in Hollywood movies and even music videos. This unique status in popular culture, has meant that the world pays attention to the US military, and it holds a particular iconic – if not unproblematic- international status.

A second way that the US context is unique, and perhaps most obviously, is that the US has one of the largest militaries in the world, with over 1.3 million active-duty service members, compared to Canada's 63,000 and Australia's 57,000 total active-duty members. The US military is heavily invested and active around the world and has heralded itself as a military leader of several international coalitions and operations, including the so-called global 'war on terror,' often dubbed the 'never-ending war'.

US media outlets also have a larger and more international audience. This not only means that the sheer volume of relevant articles during the time-period of analysis was larger for the US (976 total articles compared to 279 for Canada and 214 for Australia) but also that these articles were consumed by a more international audience than the Canadian and Australian media materials. The iconic status of the US military, as well as the international reach of US media outlets for this analysis mean that media coverage of MSV is engaged with by a global audience. US media coverage of MSV not only reflects and shapes national conversations on the issue, but also influences global debate on MSV- particularly within Western countries that consider themselves to be US allies. Major scandals, debates, and events like 'Tailhook' in the early 1990s or the 'Invisible War' documentary of 2012 become global reference points and are directly referenced in Canadian and Australian media coverage.

While I used the same methods to examine US, Canadian, and Australian media content, I recognize the unique status of the US military and media in the analysis that follows. This means that I explore US stories and narratives as both nationally and internationally significant. I also organize the book so that the US case is presented first, to set up an exploration of if and how some US narratives about MSV may have become internationally ubiquitous.

As indicated in Chapter 1, the first stage of the analysis of the 975 US articles was a framing analysis to determine the dominant frame of each article. Frames are the organizing idea, or central focus, of the article. The main frames for the US articles are identified in the chart below, with the two dominant frames being 'institution' and 'military justice'. While some articles included themes related to more than one frame, it was possible to identify a single dominant frame for most articles by focusing on how the problem and/or solution to MSV was described. This means that while a single article might mention culture and military justice, it was identified as having a culture frame if culture was presented as the main cause of, or solution to MSV. The second stage of analysis involved identifying consistent and coherent narratives, or stories told about MSV. These two stages were distinct and essential to the analysis. The framing analysis is useful to identify general categories and patterns in media coverage, trends over time, and differences in content between the case study countries. The narrative analysis highlights complete stories consistently told in media coverage, irrespective of frame. This chapter begins with a summary of articles categorized in each frame, before I outline what I see as the overarching stories that were conveyed within and across the frames. The next two graphs capture the findings from the framing analysis. The first graph (Figure 3.1) shows the number of articles that were identified as having a particular frame across the total number of articles. The second graph (Figure 3.2) shows the distribution of these frames over the entire period of analysis. The first graph helps signal which frames dominated media coverage, while the second graph signals how the distribution and type of frames that dominated media coverage has changed over time.

3.1 Frames

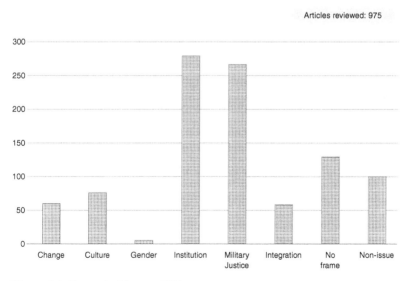

Figure 3.1 Frame incidence – USA.

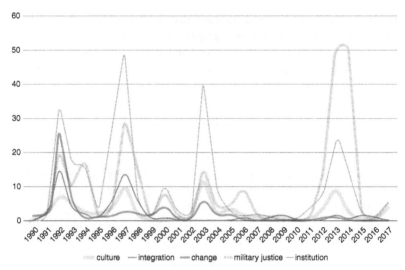

Figure 3.2 Frame incidence by year – USA.

3.1.1 (A) Change

'Change' was identified as one of the dominant frames, or organizing ideas, in media coverage. Articles categorized within this frame
tended to emphasize military initiatives or efforts to respond to MSV
or the need for change. Unlike Australia, which featured a significant
number of articles claiming proof of positive institutional changes in
addressing MSV, US articles generally acknowledged a *lack* of change
and the need for change, an expectation of change, or institutional
pressure to change, as a result of high-profile incidents and statistics
(W J Hennigan, 2014). Any claims of progress were qualified with
statements like 'We still have a long way to go' (W J Hennigan, 2014),
or offered via vague metaphor, such as 'The ship is coming in for
women in the fight against sexual harassment' (USA Today, 1992b).
It is also worth noting that, as indicated in Figure 3.2, 'change' was
identified as a frame more often in media coverage in the 1990s, and
then almost disappeared as a frame between 2000 and 2017.

3.1.2 (B) Culture

There was frequently a lack of clarity and conflation between the
terms 'institution' and 'culture' in media coverage. Some media articles

describe MSV as an institutional problem, but then prescribe cultural change as the solution and vice versa. While there is certainly overlap between these concepts, I classified articles under the 'culture' frame when they referred broadly to the work environment, behaviours, and the social norms of the military institution as the cause of or the solution to the problem of MSV. Fostering and sustaining military culture is certainly related to the institution's organization, leadership, and structures; however, culture is also something that is assumed to be shaped or shifted without altering the formal organizational structure of militaries. Articles that were categorized within the 'culture' frame tend to focus on the accepted social dynamics, norms, behaviours and practices of service members. These included training practices, hazing traditions, idealized service member traits, and informal networks or activities. Many articles within this frame attribute MSV with an embedded or 'undercurrent' of misogyny and sexism that is characterized by 'good-old boys network[s]' and toxic masculine norms.

3.1.3 (C) Institution

The most dominant frame across US media coverage was 'institution.' Again, while there remains some overlap in the use of 'culture' and 'institution,' articles were categorized within the 'institution' frame if they associate the problem of or solution to MSV with military institutional structure, design, function, history, or operations (again, this is distinguished from the 'culture' frame, which primarily includes attention to behaviours, norms, and practices). Most of the articles classified as having an institutional frame used terms and phrases to signal the systemic and deep-rooted nature of MSV, including: 'ingrained traditions', 'sustained problem', 'pervasive and intractable', (Los Angeles Times, 1992) 'entrenched', (Broder and Abrahamson, 1992) 'deeply engrained', and 'deep-rooted' (Richter and Kempster, 1997; Richter, 2000b). These characterizations describe MSV as a significant and long-standing problem that is almost a part of the military institution itself, with the implication that institutional reform[s] are necessary to solve the issue.

3.1.4 (D) Gender

Articles coded as having a 'gender' frame associate the problem or solution to MSV with a range of gendered norms, traditions, stereotypes, and expectations. Although there is clearly some overlap, these articles are distinct from those categorized as having an 'institutional' or 'culture' frame because the primary focus is on the presumed inherent nature of men and women and/or gendered norms, expectations, and stereotypes. Articles categorized within this frame link the problem of MSV to a range of perceived gendered issues, including women's physical limitations and their roles as mothers, as well as hyper-masculine warrior culture and men's inherent aggressiveness. Articles centred on gender frequently revisit women's role in the military and the perceived success or failure of gender integration. The integration of women in the military is at times presented as both the cause of, and solution to MSV.

3.1.5 (E) Military Justice

Another frame used in media articles to explain the problem of and solution to MSV, centred upon issues with the military justice system. What is most striking about this frame is that most articles focus on military justice failures, with few noting military justice triumphs or describing the military justice system as protecting victims. Within the military justice frame there are two dominant and contradictory depictions of it. The first depiction presents problems associated with the military justice problem as sporadic and isolated mistakes, rather than deeply rooted systemic inadequacies. This depiction saw the frequent use of terms like 'fumbling,' 'hobbled,' (Healy and Reza, 1992) 'bungling,' (Jolidon, 1992a) 'fuzzy,' (Schmitt, 1992a) and 'incomplete and flawed' (Goldman, 1997). By contrast, a second cohort of articles describe the military justice system as inherently flawed by design and set up to fail victims of MSV. These articles present the argument that '[t]here's a problem with the military justice system itself' and that 'the system has to change' (Stone, 1998b). These articles tend to be more specific about the nature of the systemic problem, frequently pointing to the Uniform Code of Conduct, the method of reporting incidents, and the influence of the chain of command as the core problems in addressing MSV (Richter, 1997; Jolidon, 1992b).

3.1.6 (F) Non-issue

Perhaps surprisingly, I found several articles that framed MSV as a 'non-issue', suggesting that MSV is not a significant problem and therefore no sustained attention or solutions are required. There are several ways that articles frame MSV as a non-issue, including: describing attention to MSV as 'overblown;' claiming that incidents of harassment or assault were merely jokes or normal 'rowdy' behaviour; pointing to high civilian rates as proof that sexual violence is endemic to society and not particular to the military; or having female service members articulate their positive experience in the force. What unifies these articles is that MSV is depicted as an issue that is not a systematic or unique problem or that it is a problem that is already being sufficiently addressed.

3.2 US Stories About MSV

While the previous section summarized the frames, or organizing ideas, found across media coverage, this section shifts attention to the overarching and consistent stories told about MSV both within and across these frames. As indicated earlier, one of the central goals of this book is to identify the stories we tell about MSV. My analysis builds on previous scholarship that points to the politics of public conversations about sexual violence and rape and seeks to identify any stories or patterns that might be particular to discussions of MSV. As indicated, I'm particularly interested in the ways that stories and narratives of MSV may reinforce ideals of military exceptionalism and gaslight victims and those seeking to draw attention to MSV as a systemic issue. As mentioned in Chapter 1, narrative analysis is used to identify patterns and consistent stories told across media coverage over time. Through the next section I outline five dominant narratives and draw on quotations from articles as much as possible to help illustrate my findings. I argue that these stories are repeated enough across media coverage that they seem to be taken as common sense, unquestioned and widely familiar within a public audience.

3.2.1 MSV is an Issue that Has Been Overblown by People Who Just Don't 'Get it'

The first consistent story I identified across media coverage is of MSV as an issue that has been 'overblown' by people – including activists, civilians, and politicians – who do not understand the military. This 'overblown' story has several variations. First, is the story that 'normal' fun or jovial actions have been misrepresented, misidentified, and 'overblown' as MSV incidents. Articles that reproduce this story describe MSV as misunderstood pranks, using terms like 'high jinks', 'juvenile', and 'sort of a joke' (Noble, 1994). Examples of this include descriptions of Tailhook as 'basically a cocktail party'. Similarly, another article described what occurred at the Tailhook convention as 'juvenile, but it certainly wasn't criminal ... Obviously there was activity we weren't very proud of. But there was no one raped' (Gross, 1993b). A high-profile case that involved a woman being handcuffed to a urinal was portrayed as 'college high jinks that got a little out of hand' (Simon, 1990). While these two references were from the early 1990s, the story of 'overblown' persists in current media discourse. For example, in 2017 when the 'Marines United' scandal emerged, which included a large Facebook group dedicated to sharing hate porn and unauthorized nude images of female service members, a member justified the site by arguing, 'It was just nudes', describing the page as largely a place to 'share military news and humor'.

A second variation of the 'overblown' story makes the case that the problem of MSV has been exaggerated, particularly when compared to sexual assault in the civilian context. A consistent message was that MSV cannot be described as a systemic problem because 'sexual abuse in the military mirrors all of society – no better, no worse' (Stone, 1992c). Similarly, a woman trainee characterized the sexual harassment at Aberdeen the following way: 'It's like that with any job place' (USA Today, 1996). While some comparisons to the civilian context are used to make the case that the military is 'no better, no worse,' in other instances these comparisons are used to argue that the military handles sexual assault *better* than civilian workplaces: 'Society in general needs to realize that the military reflects the morals and attitudes of society. The sexual harassment seen in the Department of Defense is 10 times worse in the private sector' (USA Today, 1992a). Another woman, former Air Force major Jeanne Holm, stated, 'Women are safer in the military than they are on the streets of most of our major cities'.

A third variation of the 'overblown' story is that MSV incidents have been handled too sensitively or in a reactive way. The assumption here is that previous scandals or broader attention to sexual assault in the civilian context has provoked unwarranted 'overreactions'. For example, one article from the late 1990s quoted a service member responding to a high-profile case the following way: 'the immediate cause of the stand down was something that would have been laughed off as campus hijinks at a civilian college or even at a service academy in *less strained times*' (Molotsky, 1996) (emphasis added). The implication here is that the broader environment has led to an 'overreaction' or greater scrutiny towards activities than is warranted.

This variation of the overblown story dominates in media coverage of Tailhook. It is important to remember that the Tailhook trial unfolded in the wake of Anita Hill testifying before Congress about the sexual harassment she experienced as an aid to then Supreme Court nominee Clarence Thomas. The hearings brought unprecedented attention to workplace harassment; Anita Hill's testimony offered unique insights into the personal impacts of harassment. At the time of the Anita Hill hearing, there was significant backlash and push back to attention to these issues and a strong sentiment amongst the public that the attention was 'overreach.' This argument seems to be an earlier version of 'political correctness gone too far' or what has been associated with the hash tag 'not all men,' in that it seeks to make the case that advocacy around sexual violence is potentially harmful to 'good men' and fuels negative generalizations about men. One article described the undue attention to the Tailhook case as 'bandwaggoning' by advocates for women who had been inspired by the Anita Hill hearings (Gross, 1993a). It is worth quoting the following op ed at length because it captures the way that the 'overblown' story in the early 1990s connected MSV to the Anita Hill case:

In the post-Anita Hill world, the definition of sexual harassment has become wildly inclusive, so that an unwelcome smile can get a guy in trouble at the office. But the events at Tailhook constituted serious sexual harassment, and the men involved should be dealt with severely. That said, the Navy may be overreacting. Last week it announced that every officer and enlisted person will be required to take a full day's training on the Navy's sexual harassment rules. Does anyone really need a day in a classroom to learn that it's wrong to grab a woman's breasts? In fact, the Navy has always had a perfectly good standard by which to judge the offenders. It's called 'conduct unbecoming an officer'. This incident qualifies for punishment under that standard. The danger is that amid the current furor, the Navy will drive its reactions well beyond the already serious boundaries of the Tailhook incident itself. It may end up setting an unrealistic and unworkable definition of sexual harassment. That may have happened at Annapolis, where, in the self-criticism that followed the hazing of a female midshipman who was chained to a urinal a few years ago, some say sexual harassment can now include merely expressing the opinion that women don't belong at the Naval Academy (Wall Street Journal, 1992).

This quote captures the many facets of the 'overblown' story related to MSV. The author acknowledges that what took place at Tailhook was MSV but argues that it is possible to 'overreact' and that ultimately, the Navy is inherently a reputable institution, and that any reforms can push 'too far'. It is interesting that the author questions women's presence and associates MSV policy changes with a reduced capacity to question women's role in the institution. The 'overblown' story, therefore, seems to be aimed at defending the military institution and resisting any efforts to use evidence of MSV to evoke systematic changes.

All versions of the 'overblown' story are crafted to defend existing institutional and cultural practices of the institution and resist efforts to initiate structural changes. It is interesting that there is an explicit connection between the Anita Hill case and Tailhook in the 1990s by those seeking to argue that broader attention to workplace sexual violence is overblown and a threat. Black feminist work allows for a deeper analysis of this connection between Anita Hill and Tailhook. Black feminists have pointed out that Black women have often been at the forefront of pushing social conversations on structural violence and that workplace sexual violence should not be treated in isolation of other forms of structural violence. Black feminists also encourage attention to blowback and efforts to reinforce hierarchies and systems of white supremacy and violence. Both Tailhook and the Anita Hill case generated national and international conversations about abuse of power, toxic masculinity, and the use of violence. Both cases drew attention to the privileges men are afforded in institutions and the forms of systemic abuse women are subjected to. These discussions provoked questions about the need for systemic changes within both the Supreme Court and the military – two historic institutions that have been dominated by men. The 'overblown' story is a story that attempts to reclaim military exceptionalism and resist systemic change by sending a message that there is not actually a problem and that the public does not fully understand or has overreacted to the situation.

This story frames any attempts to initiate reforms as hysterical and inexpert. This story ultimately positions the 'real' problem as public lack of understanding of the unique nature of the military and the series of challenges that integrating women has caused for the forces.

3.2.2 *Women Lie to Ruin Good Men's Honourable Careers*

Another story that emerges in early media coverage is of MSV allegations as lies told by bad women to ruin good men's careers and the military's reputation. Throughout media coverage a clear narrative emerged that cast allegations as a 'witch hunt' or 'fishing expedition' (Healy and Reza, 1993) typically led by women with negative motivations and 'bad reputations' designed to ruin 'good' men's careers and the honourable reputation of the military. The issue of MSV is associated with mal-intentioned women making false accusations and out of control or overreaching investigations that work together to undermine military credibility and sink the careers of reputable service members as well as tarnish the overall reputation of the institution. The investigations associate with Tailhook were frequently described this way. For example, one article described the investigation as 'a witch hunt that threatens to swamp the entire naval service. Careers have been ruined, often on the basis of mere innuendo and without a shred of due process' (New York Times, 1993a). Similarly, an article accused the Navy of a 'witch hunt' and expressed concern that 'the innocent [would be] pained with the same brush as the guilty' (Stone, 1992b). Another article that focused on the reputation of the Navy, stated: 'There are two groups of victims in the Tailhook scandal-the women who complained that they were molested, and the million men and women of the Department of the Navy who'd never even heard of Tailhook, but whose reputations were tarnished by the actions of a bunch of drunken aviators. For the sake of both these groups, we must move forward' (O Keefe, 1993).

Part of this 'women lie' story involves explicitly calling into question the credibility of the alleged victim or highlighting how the incident was misrepresented by the victim. For example, with reference to Tailhook, one article quoted an individual claiming that some women at the Tailhook conference were 'prostitutes' and other women joined in on the 'antics' voluntarily: '[u]nfortunately, there were a lot of women that gave mixed signals...There were young women who thought it was cute and funny to be manhandled by men' (Bond, 1993). Such quotes seem to justify the activities of Tailhook and imply that the accusations were largely overblown or made by women who had consented to the activity. Similarly, during the Aberdeen scandal, the credibility and motives of the victims were repeatedly questioned during the trials. Lawyers for the accused argued that the alleged victims were 'scorned' and that the Army had 'goaded them into calling it rape' (Kilborn, 1997). Convicted rapist Sergeant Simpson's lawyer argued that the accusers lied to protect their own reputation, (Sciolino, 1997) while another defence lawyer claimed the case has 'little to do with sex, sexual harassment, or the abuse of power. It has to do with revenge, reward and deceit.' Still another example is an article focused on Aberdeen that claimed '[t]he admiral's outburst reflects a growing frustration and belief among senior Navy officials that lawmakers are seizing on groundless accusations to punish distinguished officers' (Schmitt, 1994b).

In fact, one of the implicit 'lesson learned' offered from Tailhook is that large scandals can be overblown and lead to innocent men having their reputations tarnished by false allegations or by allegations made by questionable women. For example, in 1996 Cheryl Bly Chester reported: 'If we learned anything from Tailhook, then investigations into the Army's troubles will not become a witch hunt, media sensationalism and political agendas will not interfere with the truth, we will prosecute the guilty to the fullest, we will hold women accountable for their actions, and we will not persecute the innocent' (Wall Street Journal, 1996).

The 'women lie' story positions women as central to the problem of MSV and casts men and the military as the 'real' victims of MSV allegations. In doing so, this story can be viewed as an effort to preserve and restore ideals of military exceptionalism and honour, while reaffirming notions that women are inherent spoilers to the institution. Labelling victims as scorned or potentially motivated by a desire to ruin men's careers is a familiar trope that extends beyond the military. This trope runs completely counter to extensive evidence that most victims do not come forward at all, and that it is rare for individuals to pursue false allegations of sexual abuse in any workplace context. This trope is a form of gaslighting, in that it calls into question both the allegations and the character of the victim, while positioning alleged perpetrators as in need of protection.

3.2.3 If You Want Strong 'Warrior' Soldiers, Not a Bunch of Wimps, Expect MSV

A third consistent story that emerged across media coverage is one that depicts MSV as a sort of 'casualty' or unfortunate, but inevitable result of the type of recruitment, training, and culture that is necessary to create effective 'warriors,' or 'good soldiers.' In short, this story posits that creating and sustaining 'good' soldiers will inevitably lead to some levels of MSV. Essentially, there are two parts to this story. First, the military is male-dominated and defined by a warrior culture that is sometimes, albeit necessarily, toxic and sexist. Second, that women's presence, and their inherently weaker nature, may be the root cause of MSV; this section explores both.

The hyper-masculine warrior culture is both romanticized and critiqued in articles – sometimes seemingly at the same time. For example, one article focused on the Navy notes that cultural reform is 'daunting', arguing that the Navy 'has had the image of a place for hard-working, hard-drinking, hard-playing men, real men with the right stuff to go to war and leave women standing on the dock or tarmac' (Jolidon, 1992c). Another article notes that the culture of combat aviators is typified by 'the derring-do, the "drink tonight, gentlemen, because we launch at 0500 again tomorrow morning and all of us aren't going to come back"' (Abcarian, 1992). Such depictions both problematize and romanticize the hyper-masculine military culture. One article even included the argument: 'Men who may have joined the military to live out a macho dream sometimes unconsciously harass women as a means to subjugate them. By treating women as sex objects, they can avoid dealing with them as professional equals' (Shahid, 1992). Here, military culture is represented as exceptional, fulfilling men's 'macho' dreams and as fostering an environment that is hostile to women.

Across the entire body of articles, but particularly within articles coded as taking a 'gender' frame, there was an emphasis on historical and ongoing misogyny involved in military training. For example, one article reminds readers that only two decades ago the Marine Corps used the following chant in drills: 'One, two, three, four. Every night we pray for war. Five, six, seven, eight. Rape. Kill. Mutilate'. Such chants illustrate the ways that military training associates violence and winning wars with the denigration and sexual domination of women. One article explained, 'Today, the old chants are banned, but

instructors still convey a kill-or-be-killed message through intimidation and the threat of violence' (Schmitt, 1996). In an opinion article,
military training is described as a process that 'attempts to remake
the man' and includes sleep deprivation, isolation from loved ones,
humiliation and ridicule, and embracing discipline (Griffin, 1992).
The author argues, 'this kind of training is often justified as necessary
to prepare a man for the horrors of war' and asks 'what is the cost
to us all when masculinity becomes confused with brutality?' Here,
training is described as necessarily violent, humiliating, and about
'breaking down' and 'building up' a particular kind of man. While
the author asks about the potential consequences of this training,
the nature of training itself is justified as 'necessary'. Another article
quoted Gilbert F. Casellas, former chairman of the Equal Employment
Opportunity Commission and the Air Force's former general counsel:
'The military is training young men to be aggressive in combat and
face life-threatening situations, yet they also have to realize that in
dealings with female counterparts they have to switch gears.' Again,
this quote implies that military training imbues a type of masculinity
that requires a 'gear switch' when women are around (Schmitt, 1996).

Hyper-masculine military training is depicted as both potentially
problematic, but also completely necessary. The story that comes to
be told is that if the public wants highly trained and effective soldiers, they must accept some level of dysfunction in military units,
particularly when it comes to sexual conduct. The message is that the
tough training and male-dominated environment necessary to foster
'good soldiers' may also diminish soldier's ability to control their sexual 'urges;' soldiers develop an 'inner warrior' during training that
is both essential to war fighting, and also impossible to completely
control. This depiction paints a narrow picture of military masculinity
and implies that attempts to reduce MSV will inevitably weaken the
'warrior edge' and thereby reduce military effectiveness. When asked
to comment on MSV, Lieut. Comdr. Janet Marnane, stated: 'People
can't walk into an organization that is designed to fight wars and not
expect to find a few rough edges' (Schmitt, 1994a). Similarly, when
describing the fallout from Tailhook, one article argued the Navy
was 'not only struggling with practical problems of how to integrate
women into their ranks, but with a deeper military-culture dilemma:
how to teach sensitivity to trained killers. After years of instruction
about how to be aggressive and violent under extraordinary combat

conditions, these men are under new pressure to check their behaviour around women and keep sexually offensive comments to themselves' (Schmitt, 1992b).

This quote shows how effective military training is pitted against 'sensitivity training;' as a result, solving the problem of MSV becomes associated with diluting or reducing the combat effectiveness of military units. Another article captures this message: 'The Department of Defense and the service branches seem as uncertain as ever about how to eliminate harassment without undermining masculine attitudes and behaviours that many still consider essential to maintaining esprit de corps and combat readiness' (Neiberg and Schlossman, 1997). What is confounding at times is the way that warrior culture is presented as necessary for military effectiveness *and* as the source of the MSV problem. With reference to Tailhook, one narrator argued 'the abuse of women at the aviators' convention resulted from the unique stresses and warrior culture of naval aviators' (Ricks, 1996).

The story of MSV as an unfortunate by-product of a valued warrior culture paints women as possible spoilers to 'good militaries'. Articles that contributed to this story consistently questioned whether women should even be in the military. For example, an article focused on MSV noted that increased incidents had 'energized critics of co-ed basic training courses and more combat roles for women.' In response, Representative Steven E. Buyer, an Indiana Republican who as a major in the Army Reserve was quoted as stating 'The purpose of the military is to kill and break things...If you integrate the sexes at basic training, it'll depreciate the military preparedness. I don't think trainers will be as difficult or as rough on training with women there' (Wall Street Journal, 1992). This quote assumes that 'tough' training and being prepared to 'kill' are the hallmark of effective units and that women weaken both elements. What is implicit here is that women's presence is the problem when it comes to MSV and efforts to address MSV will inevitably weaken the military and it's combat capabilities. Thus, the main MSV 'dilemma' becomes determining how and if to integrate women in ways that will not disrupt the culture and how to ensure that efforts to address MSV do not ruin military culture.

In essence, this 'good soldiers might rape' story rationalizes male violence within the military as a by-product of their necessary training to be 'good' soldiers. This story legitimizes soldier violence and warns the public that good warriors cannot be bound or constrained and, therefore, some articulations of violence – including sexual violence – are not only to be expected but are a sign of a 'good' soldier. In turn, the 'good soldiers might rape' story is a form of gaslighting that not only dismisses concerns about MSV as a systemic problem requiring systemic change, yet pronounces sexual violence as a sign of 'good' soldiers and exceptional and untamable warriors.

3.2.4 MSV Is Endemic to Militaries and Women Should Know What They Are Getting into When They Join

A fourth story that emerged across US media coverage is one essentially warning women that MSV is endemic, or deeply engrained in the institution, and they cannot expect protection or justice related to MSV. There are two elements to this story, first MSV is an entrenched problem that the existing justice system cannot fix. The second element of the story includes the implicit message that women should know what they are signing up for when they join the military.

This narrative normalizes MSV as an inherent and unfixable problem in militaries and depicts the 'problem' of MSV as essentially a problem for women who are at risk for MSV and face inevitable obstacles in seeking justice or support if they experience MSV. The following quote captures this sentiment; when explaining why her superior did not file her report of gang rape in 1975, former Army specialist Barbara Franco explained: 'The whole attitude is, "That's what you get when you're a female and you join the military"' (Stone, 1992c).

When MSV is framed as endemic and unsolvable, the 'problem' of MSV is, again, treated as a women's problem both in terms of risking exposing themselves to MSV and having to navigate a dysfunctional justice system if they do experience MSV. There is, in fact, clear evidence supporting the claim that the military justice system will likely fail victims of MSV. Across all three case countries there are indications that service members have little faith in the military justice system and therefore are unlikely to report incidents of MSV. There is also evidence across all three cases of victims facing blowback and negative career implications when they report. There is also a history of cases being poorly investigated – if at all – and those cases that make it to the military justice system rarely result in prosecutions. So, several elements of this story are in line with available evidence related to MSV and justice. What is remarkable about this narrative is the

way it offers a closed assessment of the problem of MSV and the failures of the military justice system along with the warning that women
enter into such an institution 'at their own risk'.

A key part of this overarching story is the message that MSV is a
deeply rooted and unsolvable problem. Some articles depict MSV as
a problem that stems – almost mysteriously – from deep within military institutions; describing a nebulous 'undercurrent of viciousness
and violence' (Ross and Stone, 1992). A number of articles describe
an 'atmosphere of constant harassment and degradation of women'.
(Suro, 1991) a 'pervasive attitude toward women as second-class
citizens' (Stone, 1992a) and an environment of misogyny and sexism where sexual violence is 'tacitly condoned' (Schmitt, 1992c). The
'undercurrent' and entrenched military institutional environment and
culture is often loosely associated with sexism or an acceptance of sexism and sexual violence. For example, the military has been defined as
an organization rife with 'endemic sexism' (New York Times, 1993b)
and a 'cultural tolerance of sexual harassment' and described as 'an
organization built on a tradition that considers women as objects'
(Perry, 2000). This element of the story depicts the MSV as a fixture
of militaries. It is rare that specific sources of this problem, or any
potential solutions, are identified. Instead, it's almost as if the military
'just is' this way.

Another key part of this story presents the military justice system
as inherently flawed and irreparable. Articles that recognize the military justice system as dysfunction identify challenges that victims face
in reporting MSV, including blowback, having their own reputations
scrutinized, potential damage to their career or reputation, and even
counter-charges as a result of the investigation. Again, while there is
evidence to support these aspects of the story, what is unique is the
way this story seems to construct this as an inevitable problem that
cannot be solved. There is a long history within both within the military and civilian context of putting victims of sexual assault 'on trial'
by questioning their motives for reporting an incident, or pointing
to past behaviour or choices as proof that the victim is not credible
(Stone, 1998a). This can involve efforts to undermine the credibility
of the victim as well as formal charges against the victim. One article
quoted Barnes as describing a 'trash-the-victim strategy' and argued
that defence teams regularly used 'the "nuts and sluts" defense', by
focusing on the past reputation or choices of the victim rather than

the perpetrator's actions (Stone, 1997). Many victims end up being investigated themselves for drinking, adultery, or improper fraternization (Janofsky, 2003b). For example, one article describes how Marie, a former cadet who claimed she was raped, was charged for several infractions, including drinking, improper fraternization, which undermined her capacity to pursue her perpetrator and damaged her career (Janofsky, 2003a).

Alarmingly, these 'military justice as inherently flawed' articles note that in addition to victims not being believed, and being put 'on trial' themselves, there is a strong likelihood that their perpetrator will not be prosecuted or found guilty. As a result, victims must continue working within an institution that failed to protect them and prosecute their perpetrator; they may also even have to continue to work alongside their perpetrator and/or witness their perpetrator's career continue to flourish. One article quoted retired brigadier general Wilma Vaught describing how multiple aspects of the military justice system 'send[s] a signal to women that you're putting your career, possibly your life, in jeopardy if you lodge a complaint ... against somebody in a powerful position' (Stone and Komarow, 1998). Similarly, another article described a not-guilty verdict the following way: 'It's hard enough for women to come forward with complaints like this, only to find that the system doesn't work for them .... It's going to send the message "don't come forward ... If you're experiencing a problem, don't come forward, because you're going to be revictimized. Take care of it yourself. But don't try to use the system"' (Healy, 1998). Given that victims face obstacles, threats to their career, and the very real prospect that in the unlikely event that their perpetrator is brought to military trial, a court case is more likely to cause trauma and exhaustion than it is to result in a criminal prosecution for the perpetrator. The overall impression given in these articles is that the military justice system is a system in which few women bother to come forward, and those that do regret it. Navy Petty Officer 1st Class Johnna Vinson, who accused Major Gene C. McKinney of propositioning her at a conference in Denver stated: 'Knowing what I know now, unless the system changes ... I would never come forward' (Stone, 1998b). Another one of McKinney's accusers, Sgt. Christine Roy, was quoted as stating, 'What I sacrificed wasn't worth {just} one guilty verdict' (Jackson and Freeman, 1998).

The last part of this story is that victims will often be failed and re-victimized by the military justice system. Articles describe challenges that victims face at every stage of the justice system, including in seek-ing justice and support, military justice handling of cases, and the poor outcomes of the military justice system. Specific challenges described include a cultural environment in which women who come forward with allegations are stigmatized, not believed, and often face a 'wall of silence' or a culture in which perpetrators are protected by their peers. One of the most infamous examples of this was with the Tailhook court case. This case described as impacted by a systematic 'closing ranks and obfuscation' (Lewis, 1992) whereby service members pro-tected each other through silence and refusing to cooperate with the investigation. Several articles focused on the Tailhook case described how the court case was impacted by the refusal of as many as 1,500 pilots and civilians to cooperate and what was described as a 'stone wall of silence among a brotherhood of aviators who said they could not recall what they had seen at the hotel ...' (Schmitt, 1992c). An article printed in 1990 reported that 40 to 49 per cent of female ser-vice members did not believe or know whether their senior leaders or immediate supervisors made honest and reasonable efforts to stop sexual harassment, despite regulations (Schmitt, 1990).

Again, there are many facets to this story that reflect existing data and research on how military justice systems address MSV. I argue that, combined, these articles do not tell a story of the military as a dysfunctional institution in need of systemic reform. Rather, the story is that the MSV is rather naturally and somewhat mysteriously endemic and unsolvable and, therefore, women are taking individ-ual risks by joining the forces and potentially exposing themselves to MSV. Articles at times seem to mystify and describe MSV as a force beyond the control of the military. This normalizes MSV as a feature of militaries, understood as exceptional institutions. The story also places the burden for handling MSV on victims, largely women. A significant focus of these articles is on how women must navigate the military justice system and the seeming inevitable fail-ures of justice they will face. This framing positions MSV, once again, as a 'women's issue' and describes justice failures primarily through the lens of the obstacles and journey of women seeking to navigate this system. This story reaffirms overarching messages that the military is not designed for or welcoming to women and that men's violence – even illicit violence – within the military should be tolerated and accepted.

3.2.5 The Band of Brothers Evoke the 'Bro Code' and Get Away with MSV

A fifth story that emerged across media coverage is that military men will protect each other and ensure they do not face consequences for MSV. Central to this story is the message that band of brother warrior cultures normalizes sexual violence and fosters a 'bro code' of silence designed to protect perpetrators. Phrases like 'good old-boy network', (Bornemeier and Morrison, 1993) 'insular, male-dominated culture' (Suro, 1991) 'male-orientated culture' (Healy, 1992) and 'cult of the "young warrior"'(Healy, 1993) are used to paint a picture of military culture as a sort of formalized fraternity where men protect each other and celebrate certain expressions of masculinity as well as the denigration and exclusion of women.

Articles consistency described an institutional environment in which dysfunction and illicit behaviour is the norm, even against a backdrop of official commitments and policies to the contrary. For example, Rep Patricia Schroeder, D-Colo described MSV incidents as 'a reflection of the male-dominated chain of command that usually looks the other way', declaring that Army leaders 'talk zero tolerance, but they implement it with a wink–wink' (Komarow, 1996). Articles conveyed the consistent message that perpetrators felt they were in an environment of impunity. When describing the Tailhook scandal, it was noted that attendees 'viewed the annual conference as a type of "free fire zone" wherein they could act indiscriminately and without fear of censure or retribution in matters of sexual conduct or drunkenness' (Healy, 1993). Another article described the military training system as 'so flawed that wife beaters were allowed to become drill sergeants and that the enforcement of rules against sexual harassment varied widely from base to base' (Shenon, 1997). Similarly, another article noted that 'female cadets reported a culture that provided only light punishment for sexual assault and imposed a code of silence around knowledge of the events' (Hendren, 2003).

The consistent suggestion is that 'perpetrators get away with MSV,' with loose associations between impunity and a weak or unenforced set of rules with regard to MSV. As with the previous 'deeply rooted' characterization, there remains a vagueness as to who is ultimately responsible for holding perpetrators accountable and for the 'institutional failures.' 'While this story does identify individuals who 'break the rules' as part of the problem, it emphasizes that it is the institution's failure to uphold the rules and punish offenders as the source of why MSV perpetuates. This narratives depicts military culture as defined by normalized violence against women as well as the practice of turning a blind eye and enforcing a bro code of silence to avoid accountability for MSV (Richter, 2000a; Komarow, 1996; Hendren, 2003).

Another element to this 'bros will get away with it' story centres on senior military leaders. Senior military leaders are consistently described as mishandling, accepting, or relying on informal disciplinary actions when it comes to military sexual assault. In 2000 an article noted the 'considerable discretion' commanders had in how they address those accused of MSV, ranging from 'oral admonishment to a letter of reprimand that is not put in the accused's personnel file to a letter that becomes a matter of record' (Myers, 2000; New York Times, 2000). Articles recount how few allegations result in formal investigations and the ways that senior leaders who had previously faced allegations of MSV often go on to have successful careers (USA Today, 2003; Richter, 2000a). Senior leaders are also accused of inappropriate 'influence' or 'unlawful command influence' in several MSV cases, often seeking dismissal or reduction of charges (Oppel, 2014). Senior leaders are also described as facing different and weaker consequences for sexual misconduct as compared to lower ranking and enlisted members. An article described how 'top officers facing allegations of sexual misconduct [are treated] more leniently than subordinates facing similar charges,' (Richter, 1998) while another noted 'the ongoing struggle the military has had in policing sexual harassment and misconduct among the ranks, especially by the military's most senior officers' (Vanden Brook, 2017). 'Informal' responses and systematic impunity for senior officers perpetuates a band of brother culture and toxic camaraderie where perpetrators can navigate the military justice system in ways that protects themselves and each other with no repercussions or oversight.

On the surface, this story seems somewhat critical of military culture and the potential role it can play in MSV. However, I argue that there is an element of this story that romanticizes the lack of accountability related to MSV as an outcome of a valorized band of brother culture that sees men protecting each other. While there is value in considering the potential negative elements of band of brother culture and the potential toxic underbelly of camaraderie, I argue that there is also a risk to associating the problem of MSV with band of brother culture. Band of brother culture is widely revered, and unique forms of male bonding are seen necessary for military effectiveness. Therefore, if the 'problem' of MSV is understood as one of a bro code, rather than service members committing crimes of sexual violence, it may limit enthusiasm for addressing it as systemic problem because it positions attempts to address MSV as requiring a dismantling of male bonding and 'ruining' of military culture.

3.3 Analysis and Conclusion

As I noted in the introduction, the stories told about MSV in media coverage often constitute forms of institutional gaslighting. That is, the narratives undermine, call into question, or deny claims that MSV is a systemic problem requiring systemic change in order to solve it. Throughout this research, I noticed that the majority of narratives ultimately convey one of three messages: MSV is not a problem at all, MSV is a problem already being solved effectively, and MSV is so engrained in the institution that it cannot be solved. As indicated in Chapter 1, I argue that these three messages converge in how they legitimize inaction related to MSV.

Several of the narratives found in US media coverage converge in the message that MSV is not a problem. 'Overblown' narratives work to reframe MSV as an issue that has been misrepresented and mis-understood by an inexpert or overly sensitive public. Similarly, the 'women lie' narrative implies that MSV allegations are false and the product of scorned or vindictive women seeking to ruin men's careers and the military.

A second strong overarching message in US media coverage is that MSV is unsolvable. The 'good soldiers might rape' narrative presumes that effective soldiers cannot consistently be controlled and therefore the public should expect some level of sexual violence as a part of the natural expression of a good warrior. The 'MSV is endemic and women should know what they are getting into' narrative explicitly depicts MSV as inextricably part of military institutions. Understood this way, appropriate responses to addressing MSV seem to be to warn women. In addition, the 'bro code' narrative understands the problem of MSV to be one of men protecting each other. This narrative shifts the attention from perpetrators and recasts MSV as a problem of the bro code and men's unique and romantic bonds and need to uphold codes of silence both on and off the battlefield.

In addition to the ways these narratives converge with clear messages that MSV is not a problem or is not a solvable problem, another remarkable feature of US media coverage is the overt hostility to women, and the constant questioning of whether the 'problem' of MSV is a problem of women's presence in the institution. The 'women lie' narrative positions the problem of MSV as women lying, while the 'good soldiers might rape' narrative implies that 'good' soldiers are men who cannot control their sexuality and depicts women's presence as a liability, rather than men's 'uncontrollable urges.' The 'bro code' narrative also infers that women are the spoilers to men's romantic and necessary bonding. Finally, the 'MSV is endemic' narrative manages to lay the blame and responsibility of MSV at the feet of women; warning them that since MSV is unsolvable, they should consider themselves warned when they join the institution.

What is remarkable about the US case is that – unlike the other case countries – all of the narratives imply that MSV is either not a problem at all or an unsolvable endemic problem, while none imply that MSV is a problem already being handled. This is an interesting departure from other cases; as I show in the next two chapters, Canadian and Australian media coverage includes strong messages of 'we've got this' and that MSV is being addressed. For the US, it may simply be that there were so many high-profile cases and so much data demonstrating that MSV is a 'real' problem that the military was not solving effectively that the story 'we've got this' was difficult to try to tell.

As already mentioned, I argue that US media coverage of MSV has international implications. The reach of the news outlets and international attention to the US military and some of the high-profile cases have meant that the stories told about MSV in US media coverage reach well beyond US borders. In Chapter 4, I explore media coverage of MSV in Australia. Like US coverage, Australian media coverage is hostile to women and tends to present the problem of MSV as unsolvable; however, it is unique and departs from US coverage in that we see the types of debates and narratives narrow drastically.

4 | *Australian Mates*

4.1 Introduction

During my near decade of living in Australia, I was fascinated by the paradox of public reverence for the Australian Defence Forces (ADF) alongside the general lack of detailed coverage about what the ADF was actually doing, including the types of operations or the impact of their military contributions abroad. From my perspective, the international stereotype of Australians as 'laid back' and having a general perception of themselves as the 'lucky country,' are useful in understanding how the public engages with information about their defence forces. Perhaps it is this culture that contributes to a widespread sense of apathy and lack of detailed attention to their national military operations and activities. While this reverence/ignorance paradox with regard to national militaries is certainly not unique to Australia, national media coverage perpetuates this in particular ways.

This entire research project and book began with the Australian case. The initial goal of the project was to understand how it was possible that the Australian Defence Forces remained the most publicly trusted institution even in the face of multiple and ongoing scandals related to MSV. Eda Gunaydin and Umeya Chaudury, at the time undergraduate students, began as research assistants on this case study. They continued to work with me on this project for an extended time – including as they moved on to graduate studies and law school. They brought such expertise to the analysis that we ended up writing an article featuring some of the findings (MacKenzie et al., 2020) his chapter includes some of the research that we did collaboratively, including findings from our co-authored article, and I want to acknowledge both scholars for their important contributions here.

As I will discuss in the next section, one of the unique aspects of the Australian case is the fact that media coverage in Australia is almost completely dominated and owned by Rupert Murdoch. Murdoch's dominance seems to leverage and perpetuate public ignorance and romanticism of the ADF. The combination of the laid-back culture and the narrow media landscape fuels a complex and confusing set of public conversations about MSV. Compared to the US and Canada, I would summarize Australian media coverage of MSV as paradoxical, or contradictory. Every frame and story identified seemed to have two opposing messages that were difficult to reconcile. For example, military culture is often described as admirable but also dysfunctional and media coverage presented binge drinking as both a problem that can lead to MSV, but also as an important and inevitable part of ADF culture. The analysis that follows in this chapter elaborates my assessment of the unique aspects of the Australian media context, draws out the contradictions I find, and also highlights the dominant frames and stories that ring through amidst these chaotic and contradictory messages.

4.1.1 Unique Aspects of Media Coverage

As indicated, the first unique aspect of media coverage in Australia is the influence of Rupert Murdoch. The influence of Murdoch on the tone, ideological slant, and type of media coverage in Australia (and beyond) cannot be overstated. Murdoch has been attributed with changing the global media landscape, and his influence in Australia is described as 'undiluted' (Mahler and Rutenburg, 2019). Murdoch's influence on Australian media and politics is so pronounced that former Prime Minister Kevin Rudd has called for a royal commission into the Murdoch media, calling Murdoch 'an arrogant cancer on our democracy' (O'Connor, 2020). Murdoch's influence is relevant to understanding local coverage and conversations about MSV because the company is infamous for its sexism (both in its headlines and in the newsroom) and their pro-military and war stance.

Put simply, the Murdoch media empire shapes and limits public conversation about MSV in Australia. The implication of Murdoch's reach is that there is less space for independent outlets to offer alternative views on issues. Another implication is that even the few media outlets not owned by Murdoch must compete with the Murdoch-owned outlets and, therefore, seem to regularly adopt a similar style, tone, and focus. As a result, most media outlets in Australia take a more informal 'gritty' and conversational tone compared to Canadian or US media outlets. Compared to the other case study countries, Australian media coverage has more heated and passionate debates, slang terms, and a number of opinion letters that featuring incredibly sexist language and tropes.

Another distinct aspect of Australian media coverage is the unique use of language. Australians are infamous for creating slang words and shortening or abbreviating many common terms or phrases. There was such an extensive and unique set of terms found in Australian media coverage that I created an appendix of terms at the end of this chapter. The appendix includes terms particular to the ADF, informal phrases used by media outlets to describe assaults, and commonly recognized tag lines or titles used to refer to certain scandals or high-profile cases. Many of phrases and terms that were specific to the ADF are slang terms that denigrate women, or terms used to describe assault or hazing. For example, 'dully hunting' was a term used to describe older students competing to sleep with female first-year cadets, known as 'dullies.' 'Trifecta' was a term used to describe sleeping with a woman from each of the services. There is also evidence that women were regularly called 'squids,' because they are 'flabby, smell of fish, are easy to get into, enfold you with their tentacles and squeeze the moral life out of you' (Jones, 2012).

There were also terms used to negatively describe reporting assault or misconduct including 'jacking', 'dobbing' (both used to describe reporting an incident or informing on a fellow cadet) or 'crossing the road' (a phrased used within the ADF to refer to reporting incidents to the chain of command). As indicated in the appendix, there were also several terms used to describe common hazing practices, most of which involve manipulating male genitalia. For example, 'woofering' refers to a hazing ritual involving recruits having their genitals put in a vacuum cleaner, and 'roadmap' describes the practice of servicemembers holding a flashlight or torch under their outstretched scrotum to reveal the veins going through it. When it comes to ADF-specific terms, I consulted with veterans to confirm the use and meanings of these terms and to better understand those that were completely unfamiliar to me. For example, 'bastardisation' is a term used frequently in Australian media coverage – particularly between 1989 and 1999; yet, this is not a term used in Canada or the US. In media coverage, the term tends to refer to violent behaviours associated with hazing or initiation practices, primarily involving men; however, some of the activities classified as 'bastardisation' were clearly rape or criminal assaults. To me, this signalled that the term was used to diminish MSV against men and classify these incidents as hazing or initiation rituals rather than criminal assaults.

The informal terms used to refer to sexual assaults and harassment were extensive. Although Canadian and US media coverage also sometimes included more informal or slang terms to describe sexual misconduct or assault, Australian media coverage had the widest range of terms and featured informal language far more often. For example, examples of sexual misconduct were referred to as 'romp', 'bullying', 'sexual innuendo', 'sexual intimidation', 'discrimination', 'molestation', 'boorish behaviour', 'mistreatment of women', 'nude romps', (the term 'romp' was used a surprising amount of times to refer to sex and rape), 'a bit of fun that got out of hand', 'drunken misconduct', 'predatory sexual behaviour and tribalism', 'spanking incident', 'brotherhood voyeurism', 'sex without consent', 'sex pest' (referring to the perpetrator). The 'skype scandal' which was described in Chapter 2 and will be discussed again in this chapter was referred to as and 'unfortunate, sickening scenario that made headlines', 'cadet sex affair', 'high tech sexual humiliation', a 'sexual encounter', and 'friends with benefits'. The range and informality of these terms both diminishes the seriousness of MSV, but also draws readers' attention to the salacious details of the incident, rather than the criminal nature of the conduct.

In addition to the casual language used to describe assaults or reporting assaults, high profile incidents were given informal names widely used across media outlets, including the 'Skype scandal,' and 'Jedi council.' Giving incidents of MSV 'light' and 'salacious' names blurs the edges between information and entertainment, and can make the issue appear much less serious. It was useful to pay attention to language and note how informal terms diminished MSV, legitimized or made light of violent hazing activities, and painted victims and those reporting incidents as weak or problematic for the institution.

A third way that Australian media coverage is unique is the way that one incident, which became known as 'the Skype scandal' dominated media coverage and subsequent discussions about MSV (Wadham and Bridges, 2020). As indicated in Chapter 2 'the Skype Scandal,' referred to an incident that took place in March 2011 at the Australian Air Force Academy. Air force cadet, 'Kate' had sex with fellow academy cadet Daniel McDonald. She learned the sex was broadcast via Skype without her consent to other cadets the next day (Knaus and Inman, 2013). News of the story broke on April 5 and the next day Kate was brought before an unrelated disciplinary hearing.

What is also remarkable about this event is the direct policy implications. The scandal was picked up by a TV network on 1 April 2011, and days later then-Defence minister Stephen Smith announced his intention to see the combat exclusion lifted, which suggests to readers that the solution to the problem of MSV is more women. The case also generated calls for several reviews and public inquiries of military culture and management of the defence college, including two by the then Sex Discrimination Commissioner, Elizabeth Broderick, one 'cultural stocktake' of binge drinking and the use of social media, a review of the management of complaints by Defence, and a review into the way the academy handled the Skype incident. The political reactions to this case are significant for two reasons. First, they provide strong indications that enhanced media coverage places pressure on military leaders and government to respond with some indication of action – whether in the form of a policy change or call for a review. This reaffirms my earlier claim that attention to MSV largely follows a scandal and response cycle, with few political or military leaders championing the issue in times of 'non-crisis.' Second – like in Canada and the US – women's integration and questions about how women's presence in the military might aggravate or solve MSV, frequently accompanies media coverage of MSV. In Australia this was amplified by having combat roles open to women directly after the biggest MSV scandal in the country's history. For the public, the issues of women in combat and MSV were directly linked, reinforcing the idea that 'more women' or including women in different roles is a legitimate solution to MSV. In sum, the Skype scandal distinguishes Australian media coverage not only because it received more attention, by far, than any other news story but also because it was an amplified example of the overall pattern identified in the book, which is scandal *plus* media coverage *equals* official reaction and policy response/review. These unique elements of Australian media coverage are essential to situate the framing and narrative analysis that follows in this chapter. In the following section I identify several frames in media coverage, followed by an analysis of the overarching narratives I found in Australian media coverage.

4.2 Frames

In this section, I highlight the main frames identified in Australian media coverage. To reiterate, frames are the organizing focus of the article, and I selected frames by determining how the article presented the cause of and or solution to MSV. While the overall frames for Australia are quite similar to those identified in Canada and the US, the summaries draw out distinct aspects of how the problem of MSV was articulated in Australia. As indicated in Chapter 1, the distinction between frame and narrative is not always clean and clear cut. It seemed more difficult to distinguish frames and narratives in the Australian media context, perhaps because content was so homogenous, there was less expansive debate, and the messages that came through in media coverage were quite consistent. As I'll highlight in the analysis that follows, binge drinking and 'inevitability' were two themes in Australian media coverage that were difficult to categorize as either a frame or story, since both were commonly associated with the cause or solution to MSV, but also cohered, at times, into clear stories. I do not see this as a signal of methodological weakness, but a product of the useful, yet permeable categories of frame and narrative. I realise the categories of frame and story are not absolute and most readers are not reliant on these distinctions to make sense of the material. I found the distinction helpful in organizing the content and drawing out the overall patterns as well as coherent stories; however, it's important to recognize when these categories have limits.

The first chart below (Figure 4.1) signals the range of frames identified in Australian media coverage, while the second (Figure 4.2) shows

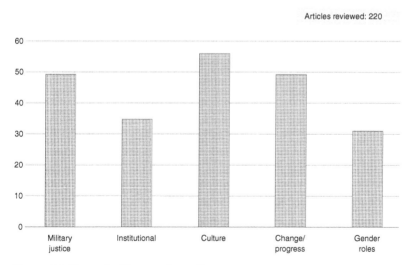

Figure 4.1 Frame incidence – Australia.

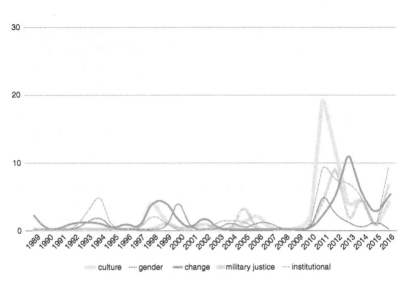

Figure 4.2 Frame incidence by year – Australia.

how these frames are distributed in the coverage over time. Following these charts, I describe the types of articles categorized in each of the frames. While the frames are identical across cases, it is interesting to note the difference in the content associated with each frame. For example, as I'll show below, Australian articles classified under 'change' were far more optimistic than US articles with this frame; these articles often conveyed a message that MSV was already being effectively handled or that recent policies were sure solutions.

4.3 Non-issue

The 'non-issue' frame includes articles that deny or dismiss military sexual violence as a problem. Non-issue was a frame that appeared in US and Canadian media coverage as well, with many articles comparing MSV rates to the civilian context, or focusing on progress or evidence that the military was handling this issue well. In Australia, most articles that framed MSV as a non-issue included either opinion pieces making general and unsubstantiated claims, or articles undermining the credibility of alleged victims of MSV. There were a significant number of opinion pieces that simply dismissed military sexual violence as a systemic issue. One such piece concluded: 'First, ... many Australians incorrectly believe that all the allegations involve serious sexual abuse, and that this was or remains pervasive in our Defence Force. Second, contrary to the evidence, many also wrongly assume that the Defence Force is somehow riddled with sexual and other abusers, or that a cover-up has allowed perpetrators to go unpunished' (James, 2012). Other articles that took a 'non-issue' frame tended to focus on individual incidences of alleged sexual violence, where the female complaint's character or honesty was questioned. This frame includes articles that suggest complainants are being opportunistic, lying, or that the sexual offence was their fault. These articles also manifest support for the 'alleged' male perpetrators for what is presumed to be a 'witch-hunt' against them. For example, in the coverage of the Skype scandal, one article noted: '... while the male ADFA cadets involved in the Skype affair should face the full force of civil and military law if found guilty, the female cadet involved is not the so-called innocent victim painted by Smith. The sexual encounter was in breach of military discipline. This, as well as the so-called unrelated offence, also reflects poorly on her 'officer-like qualities' and in the minister's own words also needs to be looked at through the prism of 'zero tolerance' (Thomson, 2012). The overall message of articles taking this frame is that MSV is not a serious issue and may be attributed to opportunistic women, or misunderstanding and misinformation.

4.4 Gender Roles

The 'gender roles' frame includes articles that associate the problem and/or solution to MSV with the unique nature of men and women. A significant number of articles offer a narrow characterization of gender roles and reaffirm an understanding of 'traditional' male-female power relationships as one of male domination and female subordination. Good soldiers are described as model men, or 'gentlemen,' and acts of misconduct as blips or occasional 'boorish' explosions of their necessary hyper-masculine natures. Many articles within this theme include quotes about how women are inherently divergent from the masculine norms of the military. This othering includes a focus on women as naturally weak victims or describe women's natural and 'rightful' place as civilians, or mothers. One article captures this characterization: 'Women belong to the category of civilians, and therefore belong to the inferior world of "outsiders"... women who provide such proof of the cadets' heterosexual prowess are described in terms which are consistently and aggressively pejorative ...' (Sydney Morning Herald, 1994). Overall, the message that tends to come through in these articles is that men and women have an inherent nature that can help explain the problem of MSV.

4.5 Change/Progress/Zero Tolerance

The change/progress frame includes articles that tend to overlook the source of the problem of MSV and focus instead on evidence of change, progress, and commitments as evidence of positive advancement in terms of 'solving' MSV. These include statements about policy, personnel, or cultural change in the military. For example, many articles discussed the introduction of 'new rules,' a 'new focus,' a 'new wave,' and 'zero tolerance' as a response to incidents and scandals. Articles categorized in this frame and the 'non-issue' frame convey a common message of MSV as 'not a problem.' The effect is that a significant portion of media coverage effectively gaslights the public, placating the public that- despite evidence of high rates of MSV- it is not a problem.

4.6 Inevitability

'Inevitability' was a frame that was not as present in US or Canadian media coverage as it was in Australia. As indicated, it was difficult to determine if 'inevitability' should be categorized as a frame or as a story. I chose to categorize it as a frame because there is not a coherent or consistent story to 'inevitability;' rather, a range of issues or factors are simply used to describe the problem of MSV as inevitable and the solution to MSV as difficult because of this inevitability. This frame includes articles that explicitly present sexual assault and violence as a normal and inevitable part of military culture. These include articles that depict MSV as an inevitable result of male-female interactions. This frame also captures articles that convey the idea that sexual assault is inevitable both within and outside of the military, given that it is highly prevalent in both civilian and military life; one article included the following statement: 'no organisation ... could expect to be free of abuse' (Hall and Ireland, 2012). Some of these articles presume that men and women working in 'close proximity' leads to assault. For example, one article noted, 'The cases I've had involving women alleging rape, it seems to be a naval thing. It could be the proximity of working relationships, the close confines' (Kearney, 2005). Other articles emphasise that service members are young and therefore apt to make poor decisions.

Partly due to the prominence of the Skype scandal, many articles focused on the availability of 'aggravators' such as technology or alcohol, as 'disinhibitors' (Jane, 2011; Snow, 2011) or factors that inevitably lead to MSV. A portion of the articles – particularly those covering the Skype scandal – point to the mere existence and availability of technology as a permissive condition for military sexual assault. At the time of the Skype scandal, then-Defence Minister Stephen Smith is quoted in an article as saying that 'people need to understand that if you go on Facebook, if you go on Skype, inevitably, these things become public' (Nicholson and Dodd, 2011). Some of the topics and themes within this frame are familiar and similar to US and Canadian coverage, however the overall framing of these as very clearly as 'inevitable' is unique to Australian coverage. Again, I chose to categorize 'inevitability' as a frame because these articles associate various elements with the inevitability of MSV in way that is often not fully explained or substantiated, with no coherent story across the articles. In fact, there is a message that 'MSV should be expected' alongside an absence of a coherent story explaining this conclusion.

4.7 Culture

Articles that were categorized as having a 'culture' frame focused on the social dynamics unique to the military that influence and normalise sexual assault. In short, these articles assumed that culture was the cause of MSV and/or that cultural change was the solution to MSV. References to culture include attention to militarism (toughness, violence, and 'warrior culture'), attitudes towards sex and minorities, drinking, hazing, 'band of brothers,' and/or group loyalty, which in the Australian case takes the form of the ideal of 'mateship', and not 'dobbing.' Drinking and alcohol abuse were particularly prominent for Australia, and are consistently framed as a 'social problem' that is rife within the military institution: 'The academy [was] disgraced last year by an internal defence report highlighting a volatile culture of alcoholism and sexual abuse...' (Dore, 1999a). As will be explained further in the next section, binge drinking was linked to negative behaviours, including 'predatory' sexual harassment, initiation rituals, and macho attitudes. In fact, drinking and the 'drinking culture' is framed as causal of sexual abuse and assault in the ADF.

4.8 Institutional

As with the other case study countries, the institutional frame captures articles that centre on the embeddedness of sexual violence and harassment in the military. These articles focus on MSV prevalence across all the services, as well as the mechanisms of the military institution that facilitate MSV or make it difficult to eradicate MSV. Similar to media coverage in the US and Canada, articles taking this frame tended to focus on the nature of the institution, including its design and hierarchical structure, as well as the history and patterns of institutional response. The following quote in an article explaining the pervasiveness of MSV captures the themes present in this frame: 'The chain-of-command structure and the rules and practice of military discipline also contribute, by allowing perpetrators to enforce silence. Loyalty to the unit, and the subjection of individual interests to that of the group can be perverted and used to ensure victims tell no one of their experience. Discipline and the chain of command, of course, are integral to the military and its operations and will not change' (The Sydney Morning Herald, 2012). Common phrases used in articles that were categorized in this theme include 'entrenched', 'the norm', 'nothing changes' 'hardly new', 'pervasive but not a problem', 'routine', 'common practice', 'widespread', 'tolerated' and 'extensive' (Wrigley, 1993; Daly, 1994b; Nicholson and Dodd, 2011; Owens, 2011; The Australian, 2011; Wadham, 2012). What unites most of these articles is the way that military institutional design, function, and history are used to frame MSV as a deep-rooted and impossible to solve problem.

4.9 Military Justice

Articles categorized as having a 'military justice' frame tend to place the causal blame of sexual assault on the military's internal justice system. The military justice system is consistently framed as inherently limited by problematic internal procedures, complaint and review processes that reward perpetrators and punish survivors, and evidence of destructions of records, and/or failure to keep records. Articles categorized within this frame also highlight the obstacles for victims seeking justice and the potential blowback or consequences for coming forward. The articles focus on the 'four Ds' that characterize the response to military sexual violence: delay, deter, deceive, and destroy. Carole Wheat sums this up when she states that, 'I would never advise anybody to complain to the military authorities about (rape). It is investigated by the military. The proceedings are in a military court and the jury are military people' (Daly, 1994c).

4.10 Stories

The previous section outlined the common frames identified in Australian media coverage. In this section, I identify two overarching narratives, or stories that came through across media coverage. These were stories that were perpetuated across themes and reinforced repeatedly over the three decades of coverage. Again, as indicated in Chapter 1 stories help make sense of complex and somewhat contradictory messages. Perhaps as a result of unique media environment in Australia and public apathy about military affairs, there was less variety in the messages and stories about MSV in Australian media coverage compared to Canada and the US. As mentioned, what was remarkable about Australian media coverage was the consistency in the messages across the range of media coverage and the clarity of the dominant narratives. In addition to clear dominant stories, there seems to be one clear overarching message- MSV is not a problem.

4.10.1 Drinking Is an Essential Part of Military Culture and Can Lead to Sexual Assaults

Over 16% of the Australian news articles on MSV referenced alcohol use, drinking, or binge drinking, with a significant portion associating the incident of MSV with an overuse of alcohol. While Canada and US coverage occasionally mentioned the role of alcohol in a MSV incident, Australian media coverage was distinct in terms of how frequently drinking was mentioned and how often it was, almost unquestionably, presented as the cause or exacerbating factor in incidents of MSV. I debated including drinking as a frame, since it was regularly associated with the cause of, or solution to MSV; however, I ultimately chose to focus on the story of drinking since there is quite a coherent and consistent narrative that comes through in media coverage that includes drinking. The story, put simply, is that alcohol consumption – particularly binge drinking – is a celebrated and integral part of military culture that inevitably can lead to MSV.

Many articles unquestionably position drinking as a feature of military culture. Drinking and alcohol abuse were consistently identified as a 'social problem' that is uniquely rife within the military institution. Following a series of high-profile sexual assaults involving drinking, Former Army Chief Ken Gillespie declared, 'Indeed, looking to our past, the army has been one of Australia's most ardent national institutions to condone if not actively promote a drinking culture' (Nicholson and Dodd, 2011). Alcohol abuse was often explicitly linked to sexual assault, as two symptoms of a toxic cultural environment. Drinking and binge drinking is linked to negative behaviours, including 'predatory' sexual harassment, initiation rituals, and macho attitudes. This association between alcohol abuse and sexual abuse begins right from recruitment and academy training. A 1999 report focused on the Australian Defence Force Academy identified alcohol abuse as the 'main cause of the sexual harassment and assaults' and described 'a volatile culture of alcoholism and sexual abuse...' (Dore, 1999b). An opinion piece in 1998 concluded that 'the ADFA culture is based on, and exacerbated, by binge-drinking' (Greene, 1998). In response to the 1999 report on the academies, then Minister for Defence Personnel, Bronwyn Bishop said: 'We are running a military academy, not a finishing school' (Sydney Morning Herald, 1998).

One article focused on ADF behaviour on deployments quoted Gary Jones, who owned a hotel that catered to ADF Navy service members. He reported that when Navy members stayed at the hotel, rooms had been vandalized and he had heard of cases of sexual harassment. He summarized: 'They hit the piss as soon as they get on the island and they are not the same people; they are different (once they have had alcohol...It's the alcohol, mate. It must be a group of people that really hit it hard and cause problems for the others' (The Australian, 2002).

Another article entitled 'Drunken troops in 'schoolies'[1] binge' noted that a Defence Force basketball tournament had 'descended into drunkenness, crude initiation ceremonies and sexual harassment... Troops cavorted in clown suits and florescent vest bearing slogans

---

[1] 'Schoolies' is a slang term used to refer to a period of intense partying that takes place when high school students finish the year – it often involves binge drinking

including "NT SLAVE" and "SA VIRGIN SLUT" [NT and SA likely referring to Northern Territories and South Australia] as part of what were described as initiation ceremonies.' The article went on to note that 'sexual harassment and drinking games were encouraged by the lieutenant colonel supervising the tournament ...' Another high-profile incident came from a report that a Navy deployment in 2009 included rampant 'drunkenness and sexual intimidation'. In response to the report, then Chief of the Navy stated 'Inevitably, this report shows us that alcohol-fuelled activity led to inappropriate behaviour. This was especially directed against women.' At the same time, then Chief of the Defence Force pledged to eradicate the cultural 'cancer' of alcohol abuse in the force. The comparison of a Defence Force basketball tournament to 'schoolies' signals wider acceptance of binge drinking in Australia as a natural and normal part of celebrating or bonding as a group. Another article explicitly connected problematic views of binge drinking inside and outside the military: 'The abuse of women is not unique to the ADF. It is rampant wherever young men gather... There ought to be national outrage at this. We have a generation where too many young men think binge drinking and contemptuous brutality towards women is just another terrific night out' (Carlton, 2011).

Binge drinking and alcohol abuse are used to support arguments that MSV is *both* isolated and systemic. Incidents of military sexual violence are framed as isolated outcomes of excess drinking. However, binge drinking is also presented as an inherent feature of military culture and a permissive or explanatory cause of military sexual assault. The overall message seems to be that alcohol abuse is an unfortunate, but fixed part of military culture that can lead to abuse. Even as articles present evidence of MSV, there is often a rationalizing or message that this evidence is not an indication of a problem. Instead, the goal of articles seems to almost be to help the public understand the unique elements of the military that they should accept alongside MSV. In this case, the public is regularly asked to both acknowledge binge drinking and accept binge drinking just as they are asked to acknowledge MSV but accept MSV.

4.10.2 Good Soldiers and Normal Military Culture Are a Risk to Women

This narrative is similar to the ' If you want strong 'warrior' soldiers, not a bunch of wimps, expect MSV' and 'bro code' narratives found in US media coverage in that it presumes a distinct and necessary hyper-masculine warrior culture that cannot always be controlled. In essence, there are two parts to this story – first, that military culture and 'good soldiers' are necessarily unique, mysterious, and not fully controllable. Second, women are positioned as potential spoilers to this culture and described as putting themselves at risk by entering military culture or exposing themselves to 'good soldiers.' This second element of the story implies that male soldiers could always be expected to occasionally 'lose control' of their sexual drive and women would always remain vulnerable to MSV, particularly given their presumed weaknesses. What is unique to Australian media coverage is this persistent overt use of paradoxes to define military culture as admirable and dysfunctional and good soldiers as honourable but uncontrollable.

Again, culture refers to the social dynamics unique to the military that were presumed to influence, condone and/or normalize sexual assault. There is a wide range of cultural elements of the military linked to MSV mentioned in the news coverage. These include militarism, toughness, violence, 'warrior culture', attitudes towards sex and minorities, drinking, hazing, 'band of brothers,' and/or group loyalty. As indicated earlier, what is perhaps unique to ADF culture is the specific articulation of elements of group culture, which is often described as 'mateship', which focuses specifically on not speaking to authority figures about their peers' misbehaviour, and sanctions sexual assault – often referred to as 'bastardisation' or 'hazing' – as a method of group bonding.

Military culture was consistently referred to both as admirable, and persistently dysfunctional. What is incredible about these articles is the way that military culture is presented at once as inherently dysfunctional and also as uniquely valuable and essential for warfare activities. In fact, references to culture were made both in arguments that sexual violence is rare and isolated within the military and in arguments that sexual violence is systemic something that the public should expect. In some instances, attention to culture described 'pockets' or groups of service members that had developed what was described as an unhealthy sub-culture of misogyny unrepresentative of wider military culture. Seemingly in contrast, articles also consistently described a 'warrior' and 'tribal' culture that inevitably breeds sexism, aggression, and violence, making sexual violence inevitable. What was striking about news coverage, was that these did not become two competing positions; rather, these arguments often worked together to create a picture of military culture as admirable, but dysfunctional.

For example, one article describes the 'tribal culture' aboard a particular naval ship where widespread sexual violence had been reported as 'misbehaviour [that] was not endemic in the navy at large, but an unhealthy culture' specific to this ship where 'many crew remained on board for many years instead of being circulated around the navy' (Nicholson, 2011). This article seems to acknowledge the role of culture in explaining military sexual assault, while minimizing the incidences of sexual violence as isolated or unrepresentative of 'normal' and honourable military culture and behaviour. The article seems to associate sexual violence with elements of the navy and services that are not likely to change, including long navy deployments and assignments to particular units and ships.

Articles focused on culture often celebrated the internal 'warrior culture' at the same time as they ascribe the military's sexual violence problem to the military to this culture. In short, it is heralded and rendered problematic in the same article. One opinion piece concluded: Worldwide, military culture is unique, and it needs to be. Teaching and training people to kill in defence of the nation and its interests is serious business and our people do it exceptionally well. [However, also] produces a culture of entitlement and an environment in which challenge and accountability are not appreciated (Fitzgibbon, 2012, p. 131). This piece seems to tell the reader that required military training inevitably provides service members with a sense of recklessness and immunity that can lead to sexual assault.

According to this narrative, 'good soldiers' are necessarily strong and macho to the point that their hyper-masculinity cannot be controlled. For example, one article written by a former Air Force pilot draws conclusions about the impact of men's presumed natural sex drive, stating that you cannot expect 'testosterone to remain dormant' when men and women are 'at the peak of their sexuality, then training them to be warriors ... and putting them together in a semi-cloistered environment' (Snow, 2012b, p. 107). This statement brings together assumptions about the inherent nature of men and women, as well as arguments about the inevitability of assault occurring when men and women work in close confines together. There are two underlying assumptions here: first, that if men are left to their own devices, they will naturally assault women; and, second, good soldiers have a 'wild' warrior internal nature that must be nurtured and can never fully be controlled. Thus, in addition to the requirement that men be 'mates' and remain loyal to one another, they are also required to be aggressive and violent, and masculine to the point of machismo (Mitchell, 2000; Furedi, 2012; Snow, 2012a; Box, 2014). In combination, these representations of culture particularly normalise MSV, by suggesting that a sufficiently bonded and lethal defence force – the military's *raison d'etre,* and the discourse underlying the 'band of brothers' trope – cannot be had without a necessary level of sexual violence.

A key part of this narrative is the depiction of women as distinct from 'good soldiers' (understood to be men) and spoilers to military culture. Many articles include quotes about how women are inherently divergent from the masculine norms of the military. This othering includes a focus on women as naturally weak victims requiring male protection, or descriptions of women's natural and 'rightful' place as civilians, or mothers. For example, this article emphasised the gendered nature of combat and the inherent drive that men have to protect women: 'There is this link between statehood and man hood, between combat and man hood. The military is all about defending our women against the external threat...For our boys in khaki...male cadet peers actively protect female cadets in their group' (Greene, 1998, p. 27). Another article captures this characterisation, stating that 'women belong to the category of civilians, and therefore belong to the inferior world of "outsiders"... women who provide such proof of the cadets' heterosexual prowess are described in terms which are consistently and aggressively pejorative' (Ramsey, 1994). The implicit message conveyed in some of these articles is that the military institution is not to blame for military sexual violence; the problem lies either with the men who commit the act, or with the women who enter the military, and with gendered conditioning which precedes the military institution.

These articles often drew an explicit link to the policy of gender integration, with one noting that the 'increased incidence of sexual harassment is seen by some as a flow-on effect of gender integration' (Green, 1998). According to this logic, men's sexual appetite is uncontrollable and therefore incidents of sexual assault should be understood as the predictable shortfall of men's sexual control. The flow on implication is that women are the biggest problem when it comes to MSV. In turn, 'solving' MSV would require either removing women, or altering their role in the military. In the wake of the sexual harassment scandal on the HMAS, for example, it was noted that perhaps women had been integrated 'too fast' into the Navy. Sex scandals have also often been seized upon to argue for expanding women's leadership and combat roles, wherein proponents argue that if this happened men would respect women more and not harass or assault them. As with Tailhook in the US, in Australia it is possible to draw a direct link between the outbreak of the Skype sex scandal and calls to further integration women, including the lifting of the combat exclusion. The Skype scandal was picked up by channel 10 on 1 April 2011, and only five days later the then-Defence minister announced his intention to see the combat exclusion lifted, allowing us to draw a clear correlation between the two phenomena. These representations isolate the problem onto men and women as individuals, overlooking the fact that the problem of military sexual violence pre-exists the integration of women into the services, and does not rely on temporary factors such as their status within the organisation.

4.11 Analysis and Conclusion

As indicated in the Introduction, Australian media coverage is unique in that Rupert Murdoch's ownership of the majority of media outlets impacts the coverage, tone, and range and type of debates in media coverage of MSV. There is also a general tone of informality unique to Australian media coverage, which includes a tendency to use slang, monikers, and quote soldiers using slang more often than US and Canadian coverage. What emerges when one takes a macro-level analysis of the coverage is an almost singular message that MSV is inevitable, but not a problem. There is a level of resignation, justification, and legitimization of MSV in much of the media articles. Toxic culture, drinking, and uncontrollable warriors are seen as unfortunate but essential parts of military life that will inevitably lead to MSV. The message seems to be that binge drinking is a problem, but it will not go away, and warrior culture is necessary but will likely lead to assaults. In this way, unlike other cases, the paradoxes or contradictions associated with MSV are explicitly acknowledged and excused.

In Chapter 5 I explore the Canadian case, which differs starkly from Australian media coverage in a number of ways. In particular, Canadian media have historically treated MSV as a neutral, non-controversial event and coverage of MSV resembles coverage almost of a car accident or unusual weather. Unlike Australian media coverage, where MSV events and data provoke a range of debates about military culture, bro codes and whether women should be in the military, as I will show in the next chapter, Canadian media has largely excluded debate and only recently began covering this issue with attention to possible causes of the problem or solutions to address it.

Appendix 1 Informal Terms Found in Australian Media Coverage and Research on MSV

Abortion	A pejorative term referring to someone who has 'no value in life.'
Atomic sit-up	A hazing practice involving recruits having their vision obscured (for instance, by a towel) and being forced to do a sit-up, usually into someone's exposed buttocks.
Bastardization	An umbrella term referring to bullying, harassment, victimization and illegitimate initiation practices, in the context of training and educational institutions. In DART report, the term 'abuse' is used to describe practices including those that might otherwise be known as bastardization.
Beer bounty	A reward of alcohol wagered between service members in relation to having sex with another service member.
Bishing	Vandalizing the room or property of another cadet with or without malicious intent. Can include attacks on the person usually associated with hosing or throwing water.
Chamber of horrors	A reference to a filing cabinet at ADFA in the 1990s containing allegations of abuse by cadets which were placed in individual envelopes and sealed and not opened again without the consent of the cadet. See Sealed envelopes. Corps of officer cadets: the term for the cadet hierarchical structure that existed at ADFA until the late 1990s.
Crossing the road	Taking a matter up the chain of command.
Dully hunting	Older students competing to sleep with female first years, known as 'dullies.'
Frat bust	An attempt by cadets to catch out other cadets who are fratting.

Fratting	A friendship (not necessarily a sexual relationship) between male and female cadets which other cadets consider inappropriate.
Gammy	A pejorative term for someone uncoordinated.
Going grey	Deliberately setting out to ensure that neither under – nor over – performance attracts unwanted staff or cadet attention.
Gotcha	A hazing practice involving recruits having their genitals pinched in the showers.
Hazing	Inappropriate humiliation and degradation of others to produce a stressful environment.
Hoser	Groveller who seeks to place him or herself in a favourable light with staff.
Jacking	Informing on fellow cadets. Putting oneself ahead of the team. Not showing the required effort. Not a team player.
Malingerer	A derogatory term used to describe cadets, predominantly female, who do not or cannot meet acceptable standards of physical fitness, academic, military, and/or social performance. The cadet may be on some form of medical restriction and other cadets perceive that the cadet has faked the illness or injury or should have recovered, irrespective of the gravity of the original illness or injury.
Nuggetting	A hazing practice involving recruits being held down while their genitalia are smeared with boot polish and scrubbed with a hard brush. Also known as 'blackballing.'
Rapid uniform change	The practice (formerly known as 'splits') in which senior cadets assemble first years and order them to change uniform combinations and reappear in the same location in a specified time. The number of changes is increased, and the times shortened to increase pressure.
Roadmap	A practice which involves a service member holding out their scrotum and holding a torch underneath it so you can see the veins going through it. Used as a form of entertainment in, e.g. the mess.
Royal flush	A hazing practice involving recruits having their heads flushed in a toilet after it had been used.
Run the gauntlet	A hazing practice where recruits run through a corridor in the dormitory and older recruits bash them with pillowcases filled with cans, boots and other items.

Squeezer	Used similarly to 'malingerer.' Derogatory term used by cadets and some staff to describe other cadets who cannot or will not reach acceptable standards of physical fitness, academic, military and/or social performance (Woodford, 1998).
Squid	A pejorative term referring to female cadets, because they are 'flabby, smell of fish, are easy to get into, enfold you with their tentacles and squeeze the moral life out of you.'
Trifecta	Sleeping with a woman in each of the services.
Woofering	A hazing practice involving recruits having their genitals shoved in a vacuum cleaner.

5 | *Canadian White Saviors*

5.1 Introduction

The phrase, 'it's fine' helps to capture Canadian culture and situate the media analysis that will follow. As a good Canadian, I have adopted this phrase of 'it's fine', and I tend to only use it in the nationally endorsed way: when things are ostensibly *not* fine. Although sweeping national generalizations have negative potential, I would say that where Australians are easygoing, Canadians are 'nice,' and put on a positive or neutral face even in chaos, disaster, or objective negativity. In short, Canadians do not like to have difficult conversations; in the face of such conversations, Canadians have a range of avoidance tools, including using metaphors, long pauses, and phrases like 'it's fine' and 'well' ('well' must be said slowly with a raised emphasis at the end). This tendency helps explain how Canadians can be relentlessly optimistic about their weather – hoping for an early spring, surprised at another blizzard – even when the weather is predictably and seasonably cold. A less innocent manifestation of this 'it's fine' aspect to Canadian culture comes through other more serious ways, including in the national resistance to and delays in addressing racism and reconciliation, and in national hesitancy to talk about military misconduct.

This tendency for avoidance and false positivity helps me to understand Canadian media coverage. As with Chapters 3 and 4, the goal of this chapter is to better understand the stories we tell about MSV and explore whether there are any consistent 'rape myths' – or widely held beliefs about sexual assault and perpetrators of sexual assault – that are particular to coverage of sexual violence in the military. This chapter begins with a brief discussion of some unique aspects to the Canadian case and media coverage in Canada, followed by the findings from the framing and narrative analysis. The first unique aspect this chapter outlines relates directly to this 'it's fine' element of Canadian culture. That is, most media coverage is presented as neutral, as if there is just data to convey and not a systemic political *problem*.

Compared to media coverage in Australia and the US, there seems to be less debate or analysis of the *politics* of MSV in Canada. Coverage of MSV focuses primarily on the available information related to a case or series of cases, with little analysis of MSV as an ongoing problem, or reflection on the causes of, or potential solutions to MSV. As a result, there is very little range in terms of framing or themes in media coverage and a significant number of articles were designated as not having any clear theme or focus. Moreover, many articles that were identified as having a 'military justice' frame, remain focused on details of court cases or information, and are largely absent of significant analysis. This is particularly distinct from US media coverage, which saw journalists regularly engage in broader debates and analysis of issues that included the integration of women, wider social attention to sexual assault, and the role of senior leaders. In short, MSV in Canada has often been treated as if 'it's fine' and the news is merely covering an apolitical event or series of events, and not a social or political problem requiring resolution.

The Canadian case is also distinct in that media coverage and public conversations about MSV in Canada were led and largely dominated by a single publication – Maclean's magazine. Maclean's magazine is a news magazine that has been operating since 1905. In 1998 Maclean's published an exposé on MSV in the Canadian Forces that featured the stories of several survivors; this was followed by three cover stories over the next two decades. The 1998 feature garnered significant national and international attention. It is important to note that the 1998 feature came several years after the infamous 1991 'Tailhook' case in the US, which was largely seen to have sparked national and international awareness of the problem of MSV in the US. Tailhook also saw the first instances of media coverage that centred the voices of victims of MSV and focused on the personal impacts of the violence. The 1998 Maclean's feature might be understood as 'Canada's Tailhook' because it highlighted both the deep-rooted and complex nature of MSV and the impact of MSV on victims, including through first-person testimony from survivors of sexual violence. For most Canadians, this feature was the first time they had access to the voices of victims impacted by MSV.

The 1998 Maclean's feature also ignited a national discussion on the military justice system, military culture, and institutional design and traditions. It is important to emphasize that this feature article became infamous not only because it brought home the personal impacts of a systemic MSV problem in Canada but also because it highlighted claims from victims that they were unable to seek justice or support within the existing system in the CAF. Referencing the Maclean's feature, one article concluded: 'Harrowing as the women's stories were, what was most shocking was the way their cases were mishandled by military authorities' (The Toronto Star, 1998). The Maclean's feature article pointed to several aspects of the military justice system that remain under scrutiny today, including how victims of MSV are often punished instead of the perpetrators who assault them, the lack of transparency related to military justice mechanisms, and how the chain of command system can be an obstacle to justice when it comes to conflict of interest and soldiers protecting each other (Anderssen, 1998; Thompson, 1998; Murray, 1998). In addition to generating national debate, the Maclean's article also had a direct impact on policy. Following the 1998 feature, the CAF declared that all cases of sexual assault raised in the media reports would be re-examined, which was an important acknowledgement of error and weakness by the CAF in their handling of MSV.

There are two elements of media coverage which highlight the unique aspects of public conversations about MSV in Canada. The first is that for decades MSV was not reported on as if it is a social or political problem requiring debate, analysis, or solutions. Second, because the media landscape is so small in Canada, it has been possible for one news outlet to dominate coverage and set the tone for the debates that followed. The implications for these elements become evident in the analysis that follows. Compared to Australia and the US, there really are less clear narratives or distinct themes to media coverage of MSV. The following section begins with visual representations (Figure 5.1) of the dominant frames and how the frames were distributed over time in media coverage of MSV in Canada between 1989 and 2017. This is followed by a summary (Figure 5.2) of how the frames – again, defined as the organizing idea of an article – were determined and the general content of articles included in each category. While similar frames – for example, culture – were identified in each case country, there were unique aspects to articles within these categories in each country, warranting a separate summary. For example, Canadian media coverage included less range of frames and articles categorized within each frame seem quite different from the Australian and US cases. Following this summary, I identify four distinct stories that emerged across Canadian media coverage.

5.2 Frames

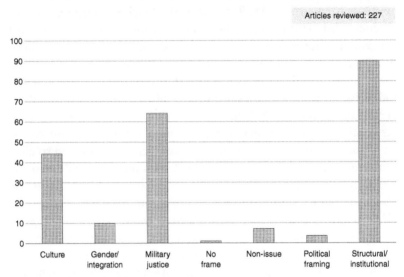

Figure 5.1 Frame incidence – Canada.

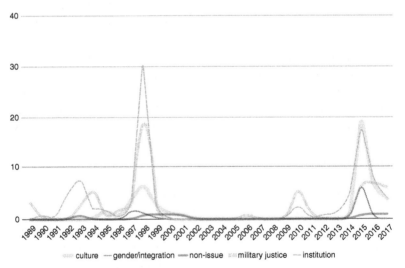

Figure 5.2 Frame incidence by year – Canada.

5.3 Institutional

Most Canadian articles framed MSV as a structural and intuitional problem. Articles were coded with this frame if they identified MSV as a problem that stems from the design or structure of the military institution, or a problem that could be solved through institutional reform. These types of articles may point to specific aspects of the institution – such as the chain of command structure – or refer generally to the problem as 'endemic' or ingrained in the military institution. In short, though many articles remain vague about the precise source of the problem or its solution, articles are clear that MSV is a problem associated with the nature or design of the military institution. As indicated earlier, many of the articles taking this frame did not provide a deep analysis of the nature of the problem or possible solutions; instead, MSV was often presented as an unavoidable by-product of military institutional design or function.

5.4 Military Justice

Articles that focused on military justice tended to centre on ongoing court cases, or the details of legal allegations or sentence outcomes related to a case or cases. Many of these articles were quite factual and designed to convey an objective account of the incident or case. This is quite distinct from articles that took a military justice frame in US media coverage. In the US, most articles focused on military justice presumed a deeply dysfunctional system and raised a number of debates and problems associated with the military justice system. As indicated earlier, it is not until 1998 that there was any criticism or regular reflection and debate about the efficacy or structure of the military justice system.

5.5 Culture

As with media coverage in the US, Canadian articles rarely defined culture and used the term loosely and sometimes interchangeably with 'institution.' The 'culture' frame is distinguished from the 'institutional' in that it includes those articles that centre on social practices, behaviours, norms, or environment of the military rather than institution design or function. Articles focused on culture tended to emphasize social behaviours like hazing or jokes, and often centred on gendered representations of activities, including those described as 'macho.' One unique term that was used frequently in Canadian media coverage was 'sexualized culture'. This seems to refer broadly to the ever-presence of sexual harassment, the permissive culture of harassment and violence, the ways that perpetrators are protected through codes of silence amongst male service members, and the cultural barriers to victims coming forward.

5.6 Gender Integration

A small but significant number of Canadian articles framed the issue of MSV in terms of gender integration. These articles associated the problem and/or the solution of MSV with women and the integration of women. Like articles centred on culture, some articles cite the masculine environment of the CAF; however, these articles also make an explicit link between MSV, 'macho' culture, and women's presence in the institution. The problem of MSV is linked to the male-dominated and masculine culture and the inability to fully integrate women into the institution. Some articles place evidence of high rates of MSV in a context of broader efforts and failures to recruit, integrate, and promote the full acceptance of women in the CAF.

5.7 MSV Stories

5.7.1 MSV Is a Complex Problem That Takes Time

The first consistent story that emerges across media coverage is of MSV as a complex problem that will take time to solve. There is a somewhat patronising tone to some articles and commentary that equates to: be patient please, this is a problem you do not fully understand that requires solutions you also do not fully understand. This sentiment can be captured with the following quote: Lawson states, 'This is a complex problem within a complex institution ... The situation therefore will require a sustained effort from across the Canadian Forces for an extended period of time. We're not talking about days and weeks, but months and years' (Blatchford, 2015). There are two elements to the 'it takes time' story. First is the message that the problem is so difficult and multifaceted that it is not known or understandable to most people and, therefore, that only a few experts can lead change on this issue. Articles that perpetuate this story describe aspects of the problem as so intensely complex and therefore impossible to even summarize. For example, one article reported that understanding a particular case required 'wad[ing] through a stack of documentation'. Referencing gender integration and discrimination, Michelle Falardeau-Ramsay, deputy chief commissioner with the Canadian Human Rights Commission stated, 'It's very difficult to change the ways of an organization like the army' (Gray et al., 1997). Other articles point to the broad types of changes that are necessary to address sexual misconduct, including 'chang[ing] a lot of attitudes' or a 'total culture shift' (Vancouver Sun, 2015).

The second element to this story is the message that rapid or incremental responses are not possible, and solutions require an indefinite but substantive amount of effort and time. Over the last three decades, senior military experts and leaders have frequently made statements that both identify MSV as a complex problem as well as assure Canadians that addressing the problem will take time. In 1998, the Minister of Defence Art Eggleton told the media that '[c]ultural changes aren't made overnight. To get acceptance in all areas of the organization of the direction we're going, takes a little bit of time' (Thompson, 1998). Similarly, in May Whitecross said. 'It's the first time we've had a team entirely dedicated to sexual misconduct and we're here for the long haul. Culture change doesn't happen overnight, it takes months and years. And we have to be there for that' (Turner, 2015). Also, in response to evidence about systemic sexual misconduct, former CDS Jonathan Vance, who was later accused of sexual misconduct, admitted the military had a 'long way to go', implying that solutions necessarily require an indefinite, yet lengthy, timeline.

What is implied in this story is that rapid efforts to respond to the problem are overly simplistic and will fail, while waiting and taking time to consider options is the preferred approach. In this way, this story legitimizes inaction, framing it as wise, measured, and rational; while efforts to initiate change are presented as inherently irrational, rash, inexpert, and unwise. 'Taking time' is equated with progress while action is associated with overly simplistic reactions rather than thoughtful plans. This story could be seen as a form of gaslighting that resists structural change by discounting the knowledge or expertise of those asking for reforms. Moreover, this narrative serves as an obstacle to structural change by encouraging an indefinite slow-down before any action is taken. This story also reaffirms a sense of military exceptionalism that presumes military institutions are complex, potentially unknowable, and require different strategies and sets of policies for addressing particular internal issues.

5.7.2 *MSV as a Systemic Force of Nature*

Another story that emerged in Canadian media coverage describes MSV as a formidable force that the military has little control over. Like the previous story, MSV is presented as a complex problem. What is distinct about this story is that MSV is described not only as complex, but as a form of affliction that has descended on the military, with no clear cause or solution. MSV is cast as an endemic problem that is 'always everywhere' without any analysis or reflection on the potential causes of the problem, or ways to address it. This reflects my earlier point about the tendency to treat MSV as an event and not a political or social problem in Canada. A number of articles point to the widespread and institution-wide nature of MSV, describing MSV 'systemic', (Bolan, 1992) 'rife', (Delacourt, 1993) and 'rampant' (York, 1993). It is noted that MSV is 'tolerated up to the highest levels of command' (The Globe and Mail, 2015). What is clear from these representations is that this is an issue that impacts the entire military and does not stem from any particular service, cohort, or group. The second annual report by the defence minister's Advisory Board on Women in the Canadian Forces stated, 'Harassment in some form has been reported by women everywhere in the Canadian Forces.'

Some articles take this a step further by overtly describing the problem of MSV as something like a plague or force that the CAF has succumbed to and cannot resist or stop. One article that focused on MSV described the Canadian military as 'haunted by sexism', while another described the CAF as having become 'a haven for promiscuity, harassment and even rape ever since women were fully integrated into the military' (The Globe and Mail, 1998). These articles seem to depict an otherwise unproblematic institution as having succumbed or been overtaken by forces that lead to MSV. Such characterizations deflect attention away from perpetrators and their actions and reaffirm MSV as a problem that is beyond the control of the institution. This story is interesting because it does not frame MSV as a solvable problem or as a signal of institutional failures. Instead, MSV is treated as an outside force that an unsuspecting military must manage. The result is that evidence of MSV does not harm the reputation of the military and there is no discussion of accountability or the source of the problem.

The story of MSV as a force of nature reinforces particular ideals associated with military exceptionalism. It likens MSV to an attack or affliction unique to the military. Rather than treat MSV as acts of violence perpetrated by individuals within the institution, this account of MSV absolves the military of responsibility and casts as just another outside force that militaries are burdened with and must 'fight.'

5.7.3 MSV Is a Source of Embarrassment for an Institution Deserving of Reverence

Another story that emerged across media coverage was that MSV tarnishes the good reputation of the Canadian Defence Forces and is source of embarrassment for an institution of which 'we' (the public and service members) are, and should be, proud of. This story conveys the message that incidents of MSV or even the 'perception of rampant sexual abuse' could diminish the reputation of the CAF or 'convince younger Canadians that a career in the forces is not respectable' (The Toronto Star, 1998). One article claimed that if MSV was as widespread as the Deschamps reported, 'it is only a matter of time before the CAF is rocked by a scandal at least as major as the Somalia Affair of the mid-1990s, something that Canada's military can ill afford' (Bercuson, 2015). The implication here is that scandals are disruptive and something the institution 'cannot afford,' potentially due to the reputational damage. Note that in this quote there is no reference to the impact of MSV on the victims; rather the attention is on how any scandal – whether it is MSV or the torture and racism of the 'Somalia Affair' – negatively impacts the institution.

Central to this embarrassment story is an emphasis on how proud service members and the public are, and should be, of the force. In one quote, Maurice Baril stated, 'I have also experienced the anguish of seeing the institution that defines who I am, and in which I take fierce pride, shaken to its core by one scandal after another' (Ward, 1998). Similarly, when defending his record on this issue, former Defence Minister Art Eggleton emphasized his pride in the changes he initiated, implying that action on MSV restored a level of lost reputation for the institution (The Toronto Star, 1999). What is interesting about this narrative is that MSV is conceived of primarily as a problem for the reputation of the institution, rather than a form of violence, perpetrated by offenders, that impacts individuals. The solutions to the problem of MSV is also seen to be centred on restoring or sustaining institutional reputation, rather than protecting individuals from violence, or holding perpetrators accountable.

This story is a powerful form of gaslighting because it erases and decentres victims and retells the problem of MSV as a problem of institutional reputation, not a problem of systemic violence. This remarkable feat of gaslighting blames victims and casts them as burdens that weigh down the reputation of the military. In doing so, military exceptionalism is also reinforced by treating the militaries reputation as precious and also requiring protection. In another sense, this story serves as a warning that allegations of MSV, and attention to MSV, might inhibit the ability of the military to recruit and ultimately do their job protecting the nation. National protection is, in effect, put at odds with the protection and support of victims of MSV. The implicit assumption of this is also that silence and avoiding addressing MSV will ultimately help militaries to do their jobs and thereby protect the nation.

5.7.4 The Military Is a Boys Club and Not a Place for Women

The final story that emerges in media coverage in Canada is that the military is a boy's club that is hostile to women. The key message of the story is captured in a quote from CAF Major-General Leonard Johnson; he describes the CAF as a 'macho and a male preserve, historically, and there were some who found it hard to accept women in the forces...' (Fuller, 1993). The first element of the story is that the CAF attracts and is dominated by men that embrace a hyper-masculine set of attitudes and behaviours. There is an implicit assumption in media coverage that male-dominated institutions like the military will 'naturally' have issues with sexism, and that these issues are amplified in the military because of the type of men that join and the training that is necessary to make them 'good soldiers.' One article quoted military college participants describing sexual harassment as a '"passage oblige", and sexual assault an ever-present risk', with one officer cadet declaring that MSV was not reported because 'it happens all the time' (Galloway, 2015). When conveying details of a report on MSV, another article concluded that 'the worst sorts of degrading behaviours are tolerated up to the highest levels of command. Women and LGTBQ members are subjected to a "hostile" environment that is conducive to serious abuse such as date rape, inappropriate relationships with higher-ranking members and enforced silence' (Hannay, 2015)

In her research on the Airborne, Thompsen argues that socialization in training reinforced values already present in individuals who self-selected for the military: an 'action-oriented profile, conservative, macho if you want' (Thompson, 1998). In an interview from 2015, then Chief of the Defence Staff Gen Lawson seemed to make the case that it MSV would naturally be present in any institution dominated by males because male soldiers are 'biologically wired in a certain way ... [to] believe it is a reasonable thing to press themselves and their desires on others' (Alleslev and Lui, 2015). An opinion piece summarizes some of the implications of the messages that men are naturally or inherently prone to sexism and sexual violence: '... the Canadian army is an institution steeped in a male ethos, led by males and employing males (with a few token women thrown in to look good). So they do dumb male things ... To train soldiers to use brute force and also to be minimal feminists will demand a whole new kind of training ... Unfortunately, what some women have suffered at the hands of some members of the Canadian armed forces is not the doings of a few but is inherent in the institution' (Anderssen, 1998). The author is making sweeping statements here about how institutions dominated by males operate. Here, the message clearly is not only that the problem is systemic, but that it is inherent and unfixable.

The second element of the story is that men (or 'dumb males') create an environment that is sexist and hostile to women. Here, the term 'sexualized culture' is used frequently. The 2015 Deschamps report described a 'sexualized culture', (Boutilier, 2015) which seems to refer vaguely to the ever-presence of sexual harassment, the permissive culture of harassment and violence, and perpetrators protecting each other through codes of silence, and a culture that discourages victims from coming forward. The report highlighted specific ways that service members were taught to devalue femininity and women. Service members reported regularly being told to 'stop being pussies' and to 'leave your purses at home', while women were called 'ice princesses', 'girls', 'bitches' and 'sluts'. The report concluded that 'the overall perception is that a "boy's club" culture still prevails in the armed forces' (The Toronto Star, 2015a). One article noted that senior command was 'responsible for imposing a culture where no one speaks up and which functions to deter victims from reporting sexual misconduct...' going on to note that senior officers were 'genuinely unaware of the extent of the inappropriate sexual conduct that is occurring..., the harm to individual members, and the damage to the CAF as a whole' (Hannay, 2015). The Deschamp report also found that women's motivations for joining the forces were questioned and uncovered a saying that women joined the CAF to 'find a man, to leave a man, or to become a man' (Boutilier, 2015).

Each element of the story is left relatively unexplored or critiqued in media coverage, sending the message that macho men, a sexist culture, and an environment that is hostile to women are unfortunate but unfixable features of the CAF. Articles conveying this story often have a tone of almost exasperation. The message seems to be that this is an exhausting problem that is unfixable. In turn, the only viable solution seems to be for women, queer, and gender non-conforming service members to simply avoid the institution altogether. For example, in an opinion piece, Heather Mallick argued: 'The Canadian Armed Forces is a terrible place for women. No, scratch that, gay males would do well to stay away too. No, change that, most men should avoid the place.'

This last narrative reflects notions of military exceptionalism that assume 'good soldiers' that are necessarily hyper-masculine and may have an untameable inner warrior that 'acts out' in ways that are unfortunate but unavoidable. This story also reinforces ideals of the 'good military' male-dominated institutions that enact legitimate violence. Women are treated as inherent spoilers to the 'good military' and men's violence within and by this institution is treated as essential and revered, even if occasionally uncontrolled.

5.8 Conclusion

The themes and stories identified in Canadian media coverage were somewhat unique compared to Australia and the US. There was a level of formality and almost coldness in media coverage of this issue. Much of the media coverage seemed to convey the message that MSV was not a problem at all, and amounted to a sort of minimization of efforts to draw attention to MSV as a systemic problem. Going back to the introduction, I view this as a move to say 'it's fine', and report details, but avoid acknowledging that things are not 'ok' in the CAF, or there is a national problem that needs addressing. The narratives I identified in Canadian media coverage also seemed to share a message that attention to MSV was shameful, negative, and harmful to the institution. It is almost as if national pride and military honour depends on evading or suppressing attention to MSV. Again, I argue that this signals national discomfort with difficult conversations and a tendency to hope to move on and move forward without having to address complex or challenging issues. In much the same way that families keep certain matters private, Canadian media coverage relays a message that attention to MSV is a violation of a national pact to support the military and nation by keeping its internal 'problems' – including MSV – private.

The implications for sweeping MSV under the carpet in Canada has been that effort to address the issue were largely absent prior to 2015 and regular and ongoing scandals have been treated as isolated. The long-terms effects of these avoidance tactics were made evident when, in 2020, the former Chief of the Defence Forces Jonathan Vance faced sexual misconduct allegations. Vance's replacement also faced misconduct allegations two months into his tenure and through the next year nearly a dozen senior leaders faced sexual misconduct allegations and several victims came forward claiming systemic problems with MSV. At the same time, in 2021 a class actions lawsuit representing victims of MSV was initiated and was overwhelmed with nearly 19,000 submitted (Gallant, 2021). The number of senior leaders facing allegations, and the number of victims coming forward as part of an external class action lawsuit signal how deeply rooted and unaddressed MSV is in the CAF.

6 | Rhetorical Tools

6.1 Introduction

This book is aimed at understanding how we have come to make sense of MSV. Work on civilian sexual violence has drawn on the concepts of 'rape myths' and 'rhetoric of rape' to demonstrate how public dialogue about sexual violence is political and signals deeply held beliefs and ideas about gender and social order. Building on this, I treat public debate and media coverage of MSV as political and reflective of deeply held ideas about nationalism, the role and function of the military in society, and gender norms. Most of the book focuses on overarching narratives in media coverage and how these narratives can gaslight attempts to identify MSV as a systemic issue. This chapter shifts the focus from overarching narratives to what I identify as a series of rhetorical tools. I use the term 'rhetorical tools' to refer to a range of language forms designed to persuade. These are tactics that are somewhat predictable, widely recognized, and often largely accepted. These tools are not complete narratives, but nonetheless use language strategically to convey persuasive messages about MSV.

The rhetorical tactics I have identified include the use of catch phrases, the strategic and selective use of data and interviews, overt political claims, and an appeal to patriotic loyalty in readers. While I do not pretend to offer an in depth and systematic rhetorical analysis, I argue that the rhetorical tools I identify align with the categories Aristotle outlined in his 'Art of Rhetoric' in that they relate to ethos, pathos, or logos. That is, they work to establish credibility, appeal to emotions, or use evidence or logic to convince. Unlike complete narratives that are well developed stories and may be identified over an extended period of time, MSV rhetorical tools are punctuations, disruptions, staccato messages that are impactful and aimed at convincing or conveying a particular message.

This chapter explores MSV rhetorical tools aimed at convincing or sending messages about MSV, as another form of gaslighting related to MSV. Again, as illustrated in Chapter 1, I use the term 'institutional gaslighting' to capture the series of tactics that institutions use to resist structural change through undermining or denying evidence and resisting critique. I argue that institutional gaslighting related to MSV often takes the form of phrases that deny the problem, call into question the nature of the problem, or make the case that the problem is being handled already. MSV rhetoric can operate as a form of institutional gaslighting that erases, diminishes, and disparages victims' experiences of MSV to reinforce and salvage perceptions of the military as a protective, honourable, and elite institution.

Through my time analysing hundreds of articles on MSV I noticed several consistent rhetorical tools – or persuasive techniques aimed at convincing or sending messages about MSV. In this chapter I begin by listing and briefly summarizing what I see as the six most dominant forms, across all three cases, before providing a more in-depth analysis of two of examples. While elements of these tactics might be used to support broader narratives or stories, again, these are not fully developed narratives in and of themselves. However, these constitute rhetorical tools because they are language tactics, strategies, and techniques used consistently over time to persuade. I argue that what unites these is that they all work together to undermine the message that MSV is a systemic problem. These tactics may reassure the public, undermine the severity of the problem, call into question evidence, shift blame of MSV to sources outside the institution, signal a lack evidence, or draw on emotion or alternative perspectives to cause a general sense of disorientation and undermine claims that MSV as a systematic problem. I list the six rhetorical tools and then provide a brief description of each. Following this, I offer a deeper analysis of two tactics – zero tolerance and statements of support from women. I chose to elaborate on zero tolerance statements because they were used so frequently across all three cases, and I felt it was important to show the systematic use of this tool. I added an analysis of statements of support for women because it was a trend that I noticed in other research projects and I wanted to understand and highlight the nature of these statements.

Six dominant forms of MSV rhetoric:

1. Calls for more evidence.
2. Referencing the service record of the accused or the victim.
3. Referencing the reputational damage of MSV allegations to the military institution.
4. Citing a previous government's failure to address MSV.
5. Zero tolerance statements.
6. Statement of support from women.

6.2 Calls for More Evidence

I identify the call for more evidence as a rhetorical tool used consistently to convince the public that 'more' evidence – often in the form of an external review, report, or investigation – is required to understand both a particular incident of MSV and the overall 'state of affairs' with sexual misconduct. Again, this is an area where published official statements and media choices are blurred. These calls for more evidence are often published without clarity around *how much* evidence is necessary, or *why more* evidence is necessary or how it might add to or change current knowledge about MSV. This is a rhetorical tool because, in essence, such calls for evidence can serve to convince the public that inaction or waiting for action is justified until more evidence is collected. It also sends a message that unclear whether there is, in fact, a MSV problem and that the public should 'wait and see' and not get concerned about MSV until more evidence is collected. Calls for more evidence, therefore, can undermine or gaslight those claiming MSV is a systemic issue and calling for action.

6.3 Referencing the Service Record of the Accused

A second rhetorical tool involves referencing the rank, service record, or history of service of an alleged perpetrator of MSV. This may include indicating that the alleged perpetrator had served overseas and/or been deployed to war zones. It may also include references to the length of service or any service achievements, honours, or awards that an alleged perpetrator has been given. It may also include references to the length of service or indications that an alleged service member had served for a period of time with honour or with no indications of having committed crimes. Research on civilian sexual violence indicates similar patterns to media coverage that attempt to paint the alleged perpetrator as a 'good' guy or normalize the person as someone who is hard working or a valued member of society. Media coverage of MSV includes particular versions of this 'good guy' rhetoric that draws on broader notions of military exceptionalism and public expectations to revere and 'support the troops.' Media coverage that uses this form of rhetoric normalizes the idea that an individual's service record is relevant to his or her allegations of sexual misconduct. This rhetoric seems to imply that a service member may not be guilty because there is evidence indicating they are a 'good' or upstanding citizen or that their misconduct should be seen more favourably against their broader commitments and work as a service member. Either way, this rhetorical tool should be seen as a form of gaslighting because it distracts attention away from the facts of a case and may enhance public reverence for both the military and the alleged perpetrator by describing the alleged perpetrator in a way that demonstrates honour, service, and exceptionalism.

6.4 Referencing the Reputational Damage of MSV Allegations to the Military Institution

A third rhetorical tool is citing reputation damage to military institutions. These include tactics that describe MSV allegations as 'battering', 'bruising', or otherwise harming the reputation of a military. The message here is that the allegations themselves are a problem and that the military is 'worn down' in having to survive the allegations. In Canadian media coverage, a more complete narrative of shame and reputational damage emerged; however, using shame and reputation damage was a rhetorical tool used in all case countries consistently. By focusing on the reputation and need to protect the reputation of the military, the military institution is positioned as the victim when it comes to MSV. This is somewhat ironic given that there is little evidence that scandals or data related to MSV have any impact on public trust for the military or its overall reputation. This tool is a form of gaslighting because, again, it positions reputational damage as the 'real' problem, rather than MSV.

6.5 Citing a Previous Government's Failure to Address MSV

A fourth rhetorical tool is a series of tactics used to put the blame of MSV on previous governments. There is evidence of this in each of the case countries. Following scandals or evidence of persistent MSV rates, military or government leaders often point to a failure to address this issue by the previous government. This failure could be described as inadequate resources, poor policy, or unwillingness to act. This is a rhetorical tool because the persuasive message is that the problem of MSV is one of a previous government's failure, rather than a systemic problem disconnected from any single government. In using this rhetorical tool, it allows current administrations and military leaders to side-step any responsibility they should hold.

6.6 Zero Tolerance Statements

6.6.1 *What Are Zero Tolerance Statements and How Do They Get Used?*

Zero tolerance statements are one of the rhetorical tools that I will explore in greater depth. I focus in on the use of zero tolerance because it is so dominant as a rhetorical tool and because there are clear patterns across all three case countries in how this phrase and form of rhetoric was used. Strong and firm statements of zero tolerance of sexual misconduct are so ubiquitous that most readers are likely to already have a strong sense of what they are. Across all three case countries, the most common form of zero tolerance statement is a formal declaration by a military leader or government official that the institution has 'zero tolerance' for misconduct or a 'policy' of misconduct. Below are illustrative statements from leaders in each country:

'The Government has a policy of zero tolerance of sexual harassment in the Australian Defence Force and we are absolutely committed to enforcing that policy,' (Middleton, 1994).

'We have a zero-tolerance policy on harassment.' Captain Marc Roleau, (York, 1993).

'We have a zero tolerance for harassment,' Pentagon's spokesman, Kenneth H. Bacon, (Lee Myers, 2000).

After noticing a number of articles referencing zero tolerance, I decided to review the entire body of media coverage with specific attention to zero tolerance to determine if there were systematic patterns to when zero tolerance statements were published, and the content of the messages associated with these statements. This meant revisiting the entire body of articles and conducting a word search for variations of 'zero tolerance', 'no tolerance', and 'not tolerated.' The goal of this part of the analysis was not to identify all uses of these phrases during this period, but to identify any patterns and draw some conclusions from these patterns. The results of the content analysis showed a high prevalence and similar pattern to the use of zero tolerance statements. The number of zero tolerance statements identified in the 30-year period were:

US: 41
Australia: 16
Canada: 44

Zero tolerance statements were almost exclusively published in the aftermath of high-profile sexual misconduct cases, or cases that received significant media attention. Following high-profile cases of sexual misconduct there was often a surge in news articles taking a 'change' frame and using a range of rhetorical phrases to signal institutional commitment to addressing this MSV. In articles where military or government officials were quoted, there was often an emphasis on the introduction of 'new rules', a 'new focus', a 'new wave', or 'zero tolerance'. The overarching message of articles relying on these phrases was that military sexual violence was something the military was 'tackling' effectively and had control over.

Figures 6.1, 6.2 and 6.3 show this clear pattern of increased media attention and then a cascade of zero tolerance statements in the weeks and months following the incident or incidents. This pattern to the timing of zero tolerance statements indicated to me that they were used strategically to respond and send a message to the public following a high-profile case. A deeper analysis of the content of these statements supports the argument that zero tolerance statements were used as a rhetorical tool to alleviate public concern about MSV following a high-profile case and send messages that MSV is not a problem, or is a problem already being addressed by the institution.

I classify the publication or reference to zero tolerance statements as a rhetorical tool because they are published with no supporting evidence to attest to the zero-tolerance commitment. The message often is that the institution has a commitment to zero tolerance, which may reassure readers or alleviate the sense of concern that any individual case or data related to MSV might raise. Zero tolerance statements did not only come in the form of direct quotes by military and government

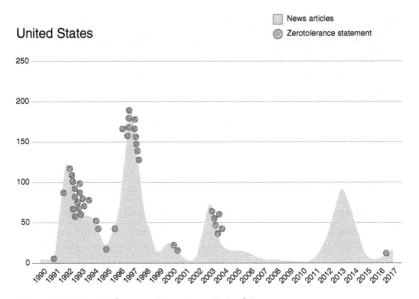

Figure 6.1 Zero Tolerance Statements United States.

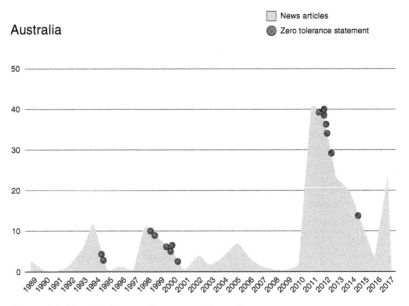

Figure 6.2 Zero Tolerance Statements Australia.

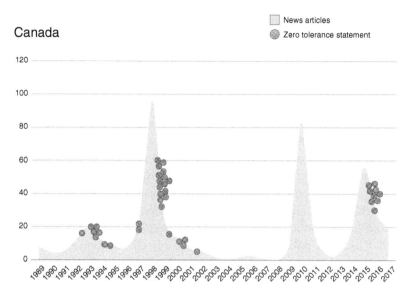

Figure 6.3 Zero Tolerance Statements Canada.

officials. Rather, journalists used the phrase to reiterate existing commitments or echo claims made by officials. My analysis includes both official statements published in media articles and the ways in which journalists use the term, often used to reinforce official statements. In the next paragraphs I provide more details on the patterns to the use of zero tolerance statements, common features of zero tolerance statements, and why I argue they constitute a form of gaslighting.

There are several features of most articulations of zero tolerance. First, zero tolerance statements claim that change is immanent. Zero tolerance references tend to emphasize the presumed progressive, aggressive, and effective responses of the military to sexual assault, and the implied positive changes the institution is making in this regard. The message conveyed to the public is that action and change is occurring. A second feature of zero tolerance statements is the confident, aggressive, strident, and even bombastic tone. Zero tolerance statements seem designed to ensure the public that 'don't worry, we have this under control.' Zero tolerance is equated with a 'tough on sexual misconduct' approach that draws on military metaphors to signal that the institution is 'tackling' the issue, is winning the battle with this issue, and has a clear plan of attack for dealing with this issue.

This echoes other forms of policy rhetoric such as the 'war on drugs', which position aggressive responses against previous 'weak' failures. The military institution is positioned as competent, strategic, and emphatically against misconduct, while the problem of misconduct is described as individual or isolated weakness or failings.

A third feature of zero tolerance statements is that they often refer to a zero tolerance 'policy' or 'strategy', yet rarely clarify what zero tolerance means in terms of specific institutional policies and practices. In addition, they often do not signal which set of policies or initiatives constitute a 'zero tolerance policy' or commitment. There is no actual 'zero tolerance' policy in any of the three case countries, yet officials in each country regularly reference such a policy. In short, the term zero tolerance policy is used consistently despite no evidence of such a policy or set of policies existing, or even any clear notion of what the enforcement of zero tolerance might look like. This affirms concerns that zero tolerance is a rhetoric aimed at convincing the public and service members of firm commitments regarding MSV.

Another feature of zero tolerance statements is that they often are made alongside claims that any service member that cannot live up to this ambiguous 'policy' of zero tolerance, can and should leave the service. For example, in 1998 then Chief of Defence Staff in Canada General Maurice Baril announced, 'Those who cannot support the Canadian Forces' policy of zero tolerance toward sexual impropriety should resign before they are drummed out' (Sallot, 1998). Similarly, following the Tailhook scandal, US Navy leader O'Keefe announced, 'Our senior leadership is totally committed to confronting the problem and demonstrating that sexual harassment will not be tolerated. Those who don't get the message will be driven from our ranks' (Melissa Healy, 1992). In 1997 when Captain Whitehead took up a new Naval leadership role he also announced a zero-tolerance policy and declared, 'Anyone steps over the line, we'll catch it – and that quick – they're out of here' (Johnson, 1997). Given that there is no zero-tolerance policy, claims that service members who 'step over the line' or breach such a policy is blatant rhetoric. In fact, as advocates have argued for decades in all three case countries, there is evidence that perpetrators of MSV are *not* removed from the service and holding perpetrators accountable has been a long-standing problem for all three militaries. So, even if we set aside the fact that there is no zero-tolerance policy, there is also no evidence that when service members breach established rules and policies related to MSV, they are 'driven from the ranks.' Instead, there is ample evidence that they will not be prosecuted, and they will be supported and protected by their peers.

Beyond the pattern of the *content* of the zero tolerance statements, there are some variations in terms of the *context* of zero tolerance statements – that is, how and when they seem to be used. I argue that there is a pattern to how zero tolerance statements seem to be used that is aimed at alleviating concerns or calls for change that may be raised after high profile incidents – to send a message that 'everything is already under control.' In the remainder of this section on zero tolerance, I outline three ways that zero tolerance statements are regularly used to convey a unified message that MSV is 'under control' or not a problem at all, these include: shutting down or discrediting evidence of MSV, signalling change and an effective strategy for dealing with MSV, and claims that evidence of MSV is an aberration of the norm. I summarize each of these briefly, with illustrative examples.

6.6.2 *Shut Down*

As already indicated, zero tolerance statements often follow a high profile MSV incident that receives significant media coverage. Going through the statements, it became clear that one of the ways these statements seemed to be used was to defensively shut down or dismiss evidence that MSV is a serious and systematic problem. For example, following a report that outlined systemic sexual harassment at US military academies, a spokesperson for the US Military Academy at West Point noted that 'The Naval Academy takes issue with the findings of sexual harassment, which are outlined in the recent G.A.O. report ... sexual harassment is not and will not be tolerated at West Point' (Schmitt, 1995). Similarly, following several high-profile cases of MSV in Canada it was reported that when a female MP raised questions in parliament about sexual harassment in the Canadian Forces, then Minister Paul Dick told her to 'stop yapping' and that the Canadian forces has a 'zero-tolerance policy' (*The Toronto Star*, 1993). There are also several examples of spokespeople or military officials making zero tolerance statements as a blanket response to detailed questions from the media about a high-profile case. For example, in 2000 a Pentagon spokesperson, Kenneth H. Bacon refused to answer detailed questions at a news conference focussed on an accused general, simply stating, 'We have a zero tolerance for harassment' (Steven Lee Myers, 2000).

6.6.3 *Change is on the Way*

A second way that zero tolerance statements are used is to signal change and instill confidence that there is a new era in how the military deals with MSV. These statements often use language of 'new policy,' or refer to a pledge, or new commitment to zero tolerance. Again, there is often aggressive language used to convey this message, including claims to be 'tackling' or cracking down on MSV. For example, former US Chief of Defence Staff Art Eggleton responded to increased media attention by declaring that 'The military is changing, there will be zero tolerance for such misconduct, give us time and you will see results' (Thompson, 1998). In his first news conference as then Secretary of Defence, William S. Cohen promised to enforce a 'strict policy of zero tolerance of hazing, sexual harassment, and of racism' (Krauss, 1997). In 2000 Australian Defence Personnel Minister Bruce Scott also announced that the Defence Forces had established 'extensive policies' to eliminate abuse and harassment and that 'Defence is an equal-opportunity employer with a zero-tolerance policy towards discrimination, harassment, sexual offences and unacceptable behaviour' (Mitchell, 2000).

6.6.4 *Incidents as Outliers*

A third way that zero tolerance statements are used is to reassure the public that any incidents or evidence of a systematic problem mentioned in the media is an outlier to otherwise normal, zero tolerance of sexual misconduct. The following quote from a former US Cadet commander captures this type of zero tolerance statement: 'I will admit that some members of the corps harbour animosities towards women, but they are a minority. The attitude does not predominate, and it has been made very clear that no discrimination of harassment will be tolerated' (Suro, 1991). This statement is illustrative of a pattern of acknowledging some evidence of MSV, while positioning this evidence as an aberration or outlier and counter to established policies of 'zero tolerance.' Similarly, following the Aberdeen scandal, Van Winkle with the Air Force Academy declared 'Such reprehensible action is utterly inconsistent with our commitment to train and equip a world-class officer corps that is the pride of our nation', and reaffirmed 'the Air Force Academy has "zero tolerance" for sexual assault' (*CNN*, 2003). Here, the ambiguous zero tolerance commitment is used as evidence that MSV incidents are not the norm; but, as there is no substance to zero tolerance commitments, this means relying on rhetoric to respond to evidence.

It should be noted that there were also several articles that featured critics, advocates, or journalists questioning the language and commitments of zero tolerance. One Canadian article quoted Professor Deborah Harrison, describing 'zero tolerance' as a 'meaningless phrase' and argued 'It's no use for Defence Minister Art Eggleton to bellow about his "zero tolerance" policies' (*The Toronto Star*, 2000). Other articles also noted or featured experts criticizing claims of 'zero tolerance' as empty and lacking evidence. For example, one Australian opinion piece focused on the systemic nature of the problem of MSV declared, 'So much for the ADF's much-trumpeted policy of "zero tolerance" on sexual harassment' (Green, 1998). Similarly, a Canadian article focused on MSV noted that '… for decades the military brass claimed to champion "zero tolerance" for such abuses, despite all evidence to the contrary' (*The Toronto Star*, 2015b). These articles show an awareness of zero tolerance as a rhetoric and an attempt to push back on this.

6.7 Statements of Support from Women

A final rhetorical tool that I identified is female service members providing a positive account of the institution or their own experience as a service member. Quite honestly, I chose to provide a deeper analysis of these statements because I recognized these types of statements from my previous work on women in combat. Asking women to show support for the institution is an interesting tactic and I have observed this pattern in media coverage about other gendered matters in the military, including physical standards and the integration of women into combat roles. I wanted to see if my sense of this pattern had any validity and understand how often these types of statements were happening and what messages they might be sending about MSV.

In coverage of MSV, these statements of support generally come in the form of interviews or public statements made by female service members or veterans offering positive commentary to counter the focus on MSV. Often in the aftermath of a high-profile case, these women would be quoted as indicating that they had a positive experience as a service member, or that – as a woman with extensive experience related to the military – they were shocked and/or willing to vouch for the military as a generally honourable and disciplined institution. I argue women support statements constitute a particularly disorientating form of institutional gaslighting because they leverage military women's voices to validate the institution, reinforce the institutions 'gender credentials' in the face of scandal or negative attention, and undermine any calls for systemic change.

To determine if there was a clear pattern to these statements, I focused my detailed analysis on US media coverage and reread all US articles looking for any evidence of women being quoted in ways that supported the institution or countered evidence that MSV was a systemic problem. I also looked for opinion pieces written by women in support of the institution and countering claims that MSV is a problem. For the US case, the body of articles I include in my data set come from four newspapers; therefore, I do not claim that my findings are exhaustive of all the potential times that women came out to offer public support of the military following negative media coverage. Nonetheless, my findings are significant and show a clear pattern of female support statements. I found 13 total clear examples of female support statements and all but one were published in the New York Times (the other being in the LA Times). The articles were written by different journalists, so this does not seem to be a signal of a journalistic choice by any one person. I argue that the results clearly show that the New York Times used this strategy of seeking out statements of support from women in their coverage of MSV.

I argue that statements of support from women is a rhetorical tool because it seems aimed at conveying a message that militaries are in fact a good place to work and that incidents of misconduct are not the norm. In fact, these interviews place a binary between 'good' and 'bad' female service members and imply that victims of misconduct are not representative of the norm. When I explored these statements in greater depth, I noticed the following three overlapping messages conveyed in interviews of other female service members: my experience is different, most military men are 'good,' and some women might be the problem. I explore each of these below before drawing out some possible conclusions.

6.7.1 My Experience Is Different

In the majority of these statements of support, women compare their own positive experience of service to evidence of MSV or in relation to a recent incident of MSV. One illustrative example is an article that includes a quote from Thea Iacomino, a 21-year- old member of the Coast Guard about to graduate from college. She is quoted as acknowledging, 'there have been some incidents ... [i]t hasn't happened to me or many other women I know here' (Weizel, 1997). This type of statement seems to position women into two camps – those that claim sexual misconduct and those that support the institution and vouch that they have never had such an experience. Consider the following quote from a freshman who had previously served a tour in the Army: 'Considering that women have been here 18 years, they've done a good job integrating the place ... I've never seen sexual harassment of any kind' (Berger, 1994). These types of statements reaffirm claims that the military is effectively handling MSV and that experiences of sexual violence are outliers. When asked about recent MSV scandals, one 19-year-old recruit acknowledged they had been 'in my mind when I signed up, but I haven't had any problems' (Risen, 2013b).

In these statements, some women acknowledge a history of MSV or some evidence of MSV, but counter this with claims that these incidents have been blown out of proportion or that things have improved regarding MSV. For example, after news broke of a male midshipman handcuffing a female midshipman to a urinal, a 21-year-old newly commissioned woman was quoted as saying, 'We're resentful of all the negative publicity that's overshadowed this week ... Most of it was blown out of proportion. I've never had a problem here' (Schmitt, 1990). This statement captures several common themes to these statements. First there is a clear message that there is no MSV problem, or that it has been 'blown out of proportion', and it signals that not all women have this experience. This message implies that the women coming forward may not be representative, or that attention to their experiences may be unwarranted. Similarly, around the same time another article featured two early career women, with one claiming, 'Everything will work out just fine ... There isn't a male–female thing here. My classmates treated me as an equal'. Later the same article quoted another woman who claimed the Academy 'has been tough, but it's been tough for everyone, not just females' (Schmitt, 1990).

In another example, Chief Petty Officer Laura Stout, a recruit division commander who had been serving for 16 years was interviewed in 2013. She recounted, 'Young women ask me all the time, 'Should I enlist?' and, you know, my niece is thinking about coming in ... 'I tell them that I don't walk around with a constant fear of being sexually assaulted' ... It is an unfortunate event that does occur. And, with this training, we will get better. So, I told my niece, "Yes. Definitely"' (Shanker, 2013). The message here seems to be a reassurance that if it's ok for her niece it should be ok for others, and that she is an expert vouching for the positive changes the military is making.

These messages appear designed to provide evidence that experiences of MSV are isolated and that some women serve with no issues or direct experience of this type of violence. Again, this tactic creates a sense that victims of MSV are exceptions to the rule of women generally having a 'good' or positive experience as service members. The following quote exacerbates this constructed divide between 'good' verses 'bad' female service members: 'not every woman is necessarily a victim ... [a] lot of these young women are very sexually active ... They have been brought up to use their sexuality to get what they want. I'm not saying the women in this case weren't raped. But we've got a different dynamic out there with our young women and our young men' (Sciolino, 1997). This quote comes from Col. Barbara Lee, who is described as having 'work[ed] on women's issues for the Army', without providing any details or clarification on what this means specifically.

6.7.2 *Most Men Are Good/#NotAllMen*

A second theme to these statements is the implicit claim that most military men are 'good guys' and that attention to MSV unfairly destroys the reputation of the majority of these upstanding men. In 2003 an article noted that 'a female cadet said she was upset by the image that the assaults have given male cadets' and quoted her as stating, 'They are being viewed as rapists and misogynists instead of the upstanding young men they are' (Kelly, 2003). Another article featured a female sociologist, who made the following statements: 'In the military, more than anywhere else, there is a potential for women to be subjected to abuse of power ... But a lot of men are supportive, and they want women to have the same opportunities they would want for their wives, daughters and sisters' (Weizel, 1997).

A lengthy New York Times feature on MSV in 1997 included attention to victims and the accused. In a section featuring accused Sergeant
Delmar Simpson, his former science teacher was interviewed and
quoted describing him as: 'a tall, thin, well-mannered youth and a
hard-striving student and athlete.' (Kilborn, 1997). After the publication of this feature, Simpson was charged with 18 of 19 counts of
rape. This same feature included extensive comments from Simpson's
mother, who said her son was 'disciplined and neither smoked nor
drank' (Kilborn, 1997). Simpson's mother also highlighted that she
believed her son was innocent and recounted a conversation with
her son: 'He said he didn't do it, and he ain't worrying about it.' In
this same feature, a Staff Sergeant who had worked with Simpson
responded to the allegations, 'I never saw any evidence of anything
like that here (Kilborn, 1997). It is not entirely clear why the New
York Times chose to write these in-depth features, or how interviewing an alleged perpetrator's former teacher and mother helps readers
to understand the case. Both the former teacher and mother seem to
be relied on to reassure readers of the goodness and humanity of the
alleged perpetrator.

In addition to the themes I draw out, it is important to note who is
asked to provide statements of support. The majority of female statements of support come from very young women – several are still
cadets, one includes a woman who worked as a recruiter, and the
above section noted that the mother of a serial rapist is quoted. It
seems strange to call on women who are only recently enlisted to add
context to a well-investigated story of systematic sexual violence in
the military. These women had little experience serving, little power
in the institution and may face professional consequences for speaking
out against the institution. It is unreasonable to ask 19- or 20-year-old
recruits to reflect on and potentially offer critical reflections on sexual violence that may harm their careers. These women indeed may
not have experienced or witnessed violence – but they also have
only been in the institution for a limited time. Moreover, a female
recruiter and the mother of a perpetrator hardly seem like objective
sources for reflections on whether the military is a positive workplace
for women. In turn, most statements of support come from women
with little power, experience, or motivation to offer critical reflections
on MSV. One cannot help but think the choice of including these
women was strategic and aimed at providing a positive alternative

or counter-perspective to evidence of MSV as a systemic problem. These statements are forms of gaslighting because they connote that only 'some' women experience MSV and imply that victims of MSV constitute an exception, or even that victims are 'bad' soldiers. These statements are also forms of gaslighting because they frame most military men as 'good guys' and, again, imply that incidents of MSV are exceptional rather than indication of a systemic problem.

6.8 Conclusion

As this chapter shows, there are important discursive patterns in media coverage of MSV that are not complete narratives, including catch phrases, journalistic tactics, and arguments. They work alongside and often feed into broader narratives to send clear messages that MSV is not a problem, or is a problem already being handled effectively. These rhetorical tools also function as distinct forms of gaslighting that undermine evidence of MSV, reinforce ideas of the 'good' military and soldier, and associate 'good' military women as those not experiencing MSV and willing to support the institution. By contrast, victims come to be cast as 'bad' or exceptional women that have been unlucky, are unrepresentative of the norm, or are lying about their experience. In sum, these rhetorical tools are forms of gaslighting that detract from efforts to treat MSV as a systemic problem requiring attention and solutions.

The power of analysing rhetoric is that it makes space to ask questions of language patterns that may be taken for granted or understood as 'normal'. I see this rhetorical analysis as a means of calling out these patterns and encouraging journalists, military leaders, and the public to be aware of them and to recognize them as forms of rhetoric. Previous work on civilian sexual assault effectively called out patterns to media coverage of sexual assault, including attention to the character of the victim, details about what a victim was wearing, or an emphasis on whether the victim or perpetrator was intoxicated. Although these practices haven't been eliminated entirely, there is some evidence that attention to rape myths and rape rhetoric has resulted in changes to media coverage and public conversations about sexual assault. For example, is widely considered unacceptable for a journalist to emphasize what a victim was wearing during an incident. These are significant changes that have resulted, in part, from efforts to call out and criticize patterns to media coverage in the past.

My hope is that identifying these rhetorical tools will be a first step towards shifting public conversations about MSV. Journalists need to be aware of these rhetorical tools and work to avoid them in their coverage of MSV. Military leaders should be self-reflective and cease using these rhetorical tools. And the public should be made aware of these patterns as forms of institutional gaslighting so they can be more critical when reading about MSV and be part of the process of holding institutions and the media to account for avoiding these forms of rhetoric. The following chapter builds on this rhetorical analysis and offers a more detailed guide and recommendations for media outlets and military institutions in how they should (and should not) frame and discuss MSV.

7 | *Recommendations Moving Forward*

This research is designed to illuminate the narratives and rhetorical tools used to make sense of MSV, alleviate concerns that data or high-profile cases might cause, and legitimize little or inadequate action in response to sexual violence within militaries. I hope to situate MSV within broader systems of systemic violence and illustrate how white supremacist ideals of the good soldier and military are central to MSV narratives and rhetoric. Identifying meta narratives and situating the problem of MSV within broad structures of systemic violence, can make it seem difficult to design a set of concrete comprehensive recommendations for how to 'fix' the problem. The main problem(s) that MSV stem from are militarism, patriarchy, and white supremacy and there are few quick fixes to these systems of oppression. Despite the daunting roots of the problem, I remain inspired by other feminist work that sees transformation as possible. Reflecting back on Sherene Razack's work, the goal of identifying national myths, or in this case embedded narratives about MSV, is ultimately to create space for unsettling these narratives and reimagining different stories.

In this chapter I identify three meta narratives that I identified as consistent across media coverage in all three case countries. I then draw out what I see as some of the core messages that come through across media coverage in all case countries. Following this, I intentionally shift from the discussion of meta narratives to an outline of some practical solutions and recommendations. These come in the form of instructions for collecting data on MSV and media guidelines for how to cover this issue. While I focus on how MSV is defined, how data is collected, and media coverage of MSV in this chapter, I see these as part of a range of transformations necessary to alleviate MSV, which should include military justice reform, cultural change, better training for military recruits on sexual violence, and stricter enforcement of existing laws related to MSV. I also see my work as contributing to broader efforts to shift public narratives about militaries with the ultimate goal as radically reforming these institutions and their roles nationally and internationally.

7.1 Meta Narratives

Each of the substantive chapters outlines several narratives that I identify in that case country's national media coverage. Taking a step back it became clear to me that there was significant repetition and some strong consistencies across the cases that I draw out here. As indicated in the introduction, I identify three overarching, or meta narratives that are consistent across media coverage in Australia, Canada and the US. These meta narratives are:

1. There are essential elements to military culture that lead to MSV.
2. The public does not understand the nature of the problem of MSV.
3. Militaries are hostile institutions for women.

In this section I briefly explore each of these, before drawing out what I see as the implicit messages that each narrative conveys.

The first overarching narrative – that there are essential elements to military culture that lead to MSV – makes an explicit connection between the presumed exceptional nature of the military and military culture and MSV. What was fascinating to me was how this linking of military culture and MSV was made unproblematic in media coverage. In her work on soldier atrocities and war crimes, Sherene Razack (2004) notes how soldier violence is excused as an understandable result of the burden of service and witnessing 'evil' in 'dark' war zones. Through this work, Razack outlines the narrative arrangements that render white Western soldiers as worthy of valorization even as they commit war crimes. Building on this, I argue that constructing MSV as an expected outcome of military culture excuses MSV and makes it possible to valorize white Western soldiers even as they commit internal violence. In this case, military training and the unique nature of military service is presented as essential and a burden for soldiers. Military training is understood to foster a fearless warrior necessary to protect the nation, and yet this warrior identity is seen as always on the verge of exploding or becoming undone. In fact, popular culture representations of the 'good soldier' often rely on tropes of a soldier that struggles to control his warrior urges and even temporarily 'loses it.'

This first narrative positions MSV as an articulation of the unpredictable, uncontrollable, and explosive nature of 'good' soldiers and warriors. In this way, incidents MSV may even be seen as evidence of the virility, hyper-masculinity, and extreme exceptionalism of 'good' soldiers. Perversely, this narrative could be used not only to normalize MSV, but also to position MSV incidents as reassurance of the exceptional nature of 'good' soldiers and 'good' militaries.

The second overarching narrative – that the public does not understand the nature of the problem of MSV – also reinforces ideals about the exceptional nature of military institutions. Here, the public is constituted not only as inexpert, but as unable to ask legitimate questions about MSV because of their presumed inability to understand the problem. I argue that this narrative can best be understood as an example of institutional gaslighting. The military is located as the masculine expert, while civilians are feminized and 'gaslit'. Black feminists remind us that institutional gaslighting is designed to resist efforts to produce radical structural change. In this case, civilian attention to MSV and questions and recommendations to address the problem are resisted primarily through presenting civilians – including academics and other experts on the military, military culture, and sexual violence – as inexpert at best, and hysterical and emotional at worst. This aligns with Paige Sweet's argument that gaslighting is a gendered political strategy that reifies existing power structures by associating those that challenge this power with 'feminized unreasonableness'. This meta narrative reifies the military as the natural and exceptional protector of social order and MSV as an internal problem that can only be understood, and handled, by internal experts. Moreover, this narrative also positions any forms of critique, questions, or attention to MSV as unreasonable, and in some cases hysterical overreaction fuelled by ignorance and feminine irrationality. The remarkable outcome of this gaslighting narrative, is that data, expert analysis, and broader attention to MSV is dismissed, rendered illegitimate, and even used as proof that the 'real' and serious, rational, MSV experts are internal to the military.

The third overarching narrative I identified is that militaries are hostile institutions for women. This narrative comes through explicitly and implicitly across a great deal of media coverage in all three case countries. In fact, the notion that militaries are hostile places for women is often assumed or taken for granted as obvious and indisputable in media coverage. One of implications of this narrative is that the military is reified as a masculine, necessarily male-dominated institution, with women as inherent 'spoilers' and at-risk interlopers. Articulations of this narrative rarely question or problematize the 'risky' male environment of the military. Instead, ideals of military exceptionalism and the 'good' military as requiring a violent and macho all-male environment is normalized. Another implication is that the 'problem' of MSV is a problem of women's presence and the risk they have taken on by joining an unavoidably hyper-masculine environment. Solving MSV, according to this logic, requires controlling, limiting, or warning women about the unavoidable perils of joining such an exceptional and masculine institution. This narrative also reframes MSV incidents as 'women's fault.' Women are questioned or even blamed for not fully understanding or heeding the warnings they have been given about military institutions. Again, this narrative normalizes internal violence in militaries and normalizes questions about whether women should even be in the military and why women would 'put themselves' at such risk by choosing the military as a career.

7.2 Implicit Messages

These three meta narratives gaslight evidence about MSV as a systemic problem and vilify female service members while valorizing and normalizing a violent and hyper-masculine institution. The narratives not only effectively resist attempts to enact systemic change or point to internal problems, but also fortify notions of military exceptionalism and the 'good' soldier and military as necessarily masculine and exerting legitimate and potentially uncontrolled violence. These meta narratives close out space for critique, action, and recommendations by presenting the 'problem' of MSV as something most civilians do not fully understand or as a phenomenon that is an inevitable part of 'good' militaries. In essence, solutions to the problem of MSV could even be understood as potential threats to the revered military culture and, ultimately, to national and international security. The power of these narratives is that MSV can be reconstituted as a sign that militaries are functioning properly, while solutions to MSV are framed as security threats. I argue that inaction on MSV has been justified, in part, as a result of the salience of these narratives. Solutions or efforts to respond to MSV are treated either as hysterical efforts of inexpert civilians or actions that could undermine critical military training and culture in ways that would ultimately reduce national and international security. Inspired by Sherene Razack's work, I argue that any effort to expose national myths and narratives must also work to unravel and move past these embedded stories and to imagine possibilities. In the remainder of the chapter, I shift from my analysis of narratives – or how we have been talking about MSV – to specific recommendations for how we *might* talk about MSV. Focusing primarily on media coverage and research, I construct a guide for those that want to change the conversation about MSV, move beyond existing narratives, and create space for alternative conversations, solutions, and understandings of this problem.

7.3 Recommendations

7.3.1 Definitions

Sexual violence in militaries should be treated as an international problem and, therefore, countries should work together to set a universal definition for this crime. This would allow countries to collect consistent data that is comparable internationally. Given how often militaries work in coalitions, as well as the participation of national militaries in international alliances like NATO or their contributions to United Nations peacekeeping forces, it is necessary to have an agreed-upon understanding of what constitutes sexual violence, how to collect data on this crime, and how it should be responded to.

As part of this effort to create a universal definition, the term 'sexual misconduct' should be eradicated in all militaries that currently use it, including Australia and Canada. Sexual violence is not merely a form of violence that violates a military code of conduct, it impacts victims and survivors. Shifting the definition away from 'misconduct' is an important step towards centring victims and aligning military and civilian definitions.

My recommendation is to use military sexual violence as a term that captures all forms of sexual violence and treats each as a serious problem requiring attention. I do not recommend maintaining separate categories for sexual harassment, sexual assault, and aggravated sexual assault because such distinctions can reinforce a sense of a hierarchy of abuses that corresponds with a hierarchy of impacts. These are not victim-centric definitions and ignore the ways that all forms of sexual violence can deeply impact victims and contribute to an overall hostile work culture.

7.3.2 Data Collection

There are some basic efforts that all national militaries and governments could make to collect better data, which would contribute to a more complete understanding of the problem and thereby contribute to efforts to reduce MSV. It is important for all national militaries to use incident reports and surveys in order to provide victims with outlets for reporting experiences of violence anonymously. As indicated in earlier chapters, the use of incident reports and anonymous surveys provides militaries with a more complete view of the problem of MSV and the potential gap between reported rates and actual number of incidents. Having a more clear picture of this gap provides militaries with the opportunity to investigate why victims might not be reporting. Partly due to evidence that victims wanted more options for seeking support anonymously after sexual violence, the US developed the option of restricted or unrestricted reporting. Currently, the majority of victims of MSV in the US initially make a restricted report, which shows that victims appreciate these avenues and will use them.

It is not enough to simply have surveys and incident reports. The surveys and incident reporting mechanisms must be consistent, comprehensive, and publicly available. US annual reports on sexual violence and their methods of conducting surveys should be seen as models of data collection because of the comprehensive nature of the data they collect, including the location of incidents, rank and service of perpetrator and victim, as well as distinct data for military colleges and training academies. In addition to this data, national militaries should collect and make public the following data: number of service members facing allegations and currently under investigation, conviction rates and punishments given to perpetrators, reasons for lack of conviction, and career trajectory for victims and perpetrators following incidents. Although comprehensive data is important, it is not a solution in and of itself. The US military has collected much better data on MSV since 2016; however, rates of MSV have gone up consistently since that time. This is a testament to the fact that comprehensive data is just the start of an effective plan and must inform a range of strategies to address MSV.

7.4 Media Guidelines for Covering MSV

As with civilian cases, there should be established guidelines for how media outlets cover incidents of sexual violence and harassment in the military. In this section I outline what I see as important elements of such guidelines in the form of some essential 'dos' and 'don'ts'

7.4.1 Don't

1. Centre the reputation of the military or perpetrator. Do not mention the alleged perpetrator's years of service, service record, deployments, record of their unit, leadership history or any other aspect of their service not directly related to the alleged incident of sexual violence. Rank can be useful to mention in order to clarify whether the incident involved an abuse of power.
2. Attempt to provide an alternative or balanced perspective on MSV by interviewing other service members who say they have never experienced MSV. Especially avoid asking early career service members, who may not have the experience or power to effectively assess the problem of MSV. These statements may be designed to offer an 'alternative view,' but they undermine victim voices and perpetuate the idea that victims of MSV are unique, unfortunate, or have an experience outside the 'norm.' To provide a comparison, if an article featured an incident of sexual assault experienced by a nurse, it would seem absurd to include statements from other nurses or medical staff claiming they have never been assaulted.
3. Don't publish military press releases verbatim. Researchers have argued that military organizations have vested interest in managing and using public attention to their benefit to mitigate negative attention and amplify positive attention. Press releases demand follow up questions and research to ensure that the full context is included. Journalists should talk to academics, non-profits or other knowledgeable sources to provide balance and context to any military press release.
4. Don't use the term 'zero tolerance'. Journalists seem to use the term 'zero tolerance' nearly as often as military and defence leaders. The terms 'zero tolerance' and 'zero tolerance policy' are used as if these things actually exist. Zero tolerance is a rhetoric: there is no such thing as a zero tolerance policy and no military I am aware of enforces or clarifies what it actually means by zero tolerance.

5. Ensure that reporters who regularly cover military or defence have some distance from military public affairs officers (PAOs). Friendships between journalists and PAOs can naturally develop, which can be mutually useful but also inhibit balanced reporting. I have observed several journalists – all men – that have embedded with militaries or worked closely with soldiers and then seemed to see themselves as 'one of the bros'. Subsequently, their coverage of the institution lacked critical reflection and often presented a positive or even romantic coverage of military affairs.

7.4.2 Do

1. Put scandals in context with data that can inform the public about trends related to MSV. Very few articles I analysed included any data about MSV to help the reader understand whether incidents were outliers or reflective of wider trends. Although the data that militaries collect is often limited, it can be shared with the public to help inform them of the systematic nature of MSV.
2. Ask follow-up questions when leaders offer zero tolerance statement or reference zero tolerance policies. Examples of such questions might include: Can you point me to the zero-tolerance policy – where is it enshrined and how is it enforced?
3. Use professional and victim-centered language to describe incidents and alleged incidents of sexual assault. There is no such thing as non-consensual sex: it is rape and should be described as such in headlines and articles. Also, click bait headlines that use terms like 'sex romp,' 'sex/date gone bad,' or 'sex pest' (to name only a few of the outrageous headlines I viewed) diminish the severity and do not reflect the criminal nature of the incident. Moreover, these headlines liken sexual violence to a 'bad' or 'unlucky' date, which shifts blame towards the victim for being in the 'wrong place at the wrong time.'
4. Write follow up stories to 'scandals.' If there is significant attention given to a particular incident, write follow up stories to let the public know what happens or what is the ultimate outcome of such incidents. Often, media coverage of 'scandals' can focus on the salacious details and the public is left uninformed about if and how the case progresses and what ultimately happens to the victim and or alleged perpetrator. This type of follow up could

provide the public with a sense of how the military justice system works and help debunk ongoing perceptions that 'women lie' to ruin men's careers. Data shows that most incidents of MSV are not reported and that, of those reported, few are brought to trial, and of those, few result in convictions. For example, the Australian Defence Forces reported 187 incidents of sexual assault in 2018. Of those, only nine cases proceeded to military trial, five with guilty outcomes, three with not guilty, and one held in abeyance due to a technical issue. Two cases resulted in administrative or disciplinary action at the unit level. This type of information and follow-up stories to scandals and high-profile cases might illustrate – through personal cases – how MSV impacts victims and perpetrators in the medium and long term.

8 | Conclusion

Good soldiers don't rape is, in many ways, the answer to the main question of this book: how do we talk about MSV? The statement contradicts and unsettles many of the established narratives about MSV. Most of the narratives I identify in my analysis present MSV as an 'overblown' problem that is both inevitable, but also 'under control' and ultimately associated with women's presence in a male-dominated elite and necessarily hyper-masculine environment. MSV is rarely described as an act perpetrated by regular, 'good' soldiers; instead, it is described as an *effect*, an unfortunate outcome of an intense work environment or women's disruption to the band of brothers. The way we talk about MSV absolves 'good' soldiers of any responsibility for the regular, predictable, and high rates of MSV. The way we talk about MSV presents incidents of MSV as a by-product of the necessarily hyper-masculine, highly unique, and intense nature of military culture and work. The way we talk about MSV places the burden of MSV on women and renders any efforts to reduce MSV as hysterical and inexpert.

The main goal of this book was to better understand how we talk about military sexual violence. That is, I wanted to understand the stories that are told about MSV and how those stories might help explain or shed light on what I see as contradictions, or paradoxes, related to MSV. The contradiction that inspired the book was the fact that regular, predictable, and ample evidence of MSV as a serious internal problem to militaries seemed to have little or no impact on public trust of the institution, or the general perception of militaries as orderly and disciplined institutions made up of highly trained soldiers with dedicated camaraderie, protecting each other and the nation. Another contradiction was that the #MeToo movement and broader efforts to raise awareness of rape culture, workplace sexual violence, and war-related sexual violence had largely avoided discussing sexual violence within military institutions. I am convinced that understanding how

MSV is talked about can shed light on broader debates about rape culture and the #MeToo movement. Militaries are the most revered public institution in most Western countries and understood to be the masculine protectors of a feminized civilian population. Therefore, understanding how MSV is described and potentially normalized can tell us a lot about wider national gender norms and values.

I chose to focus on media coverage of MSV because media attention is one of the primary means through which the public comes to know about MSV. We know from media coverage of civilian sexual assault that the types of narratives, tropes, and 'rape myths' used in media coverage have had vast impacts, including in terms of shaping public perceptions about sexual violence, influencing police reporting and court cases, and effecting whether victims chose to report or not. It seemed important to me to understand if there were particular rape myths, consistent narratives, tropes, and forms of rhetoric unique to media coverage of MSV that might also have expansive impacts.

Media coverage was an effective source for examining the stories we tell about MSV. As I indicated in the introduction, I do not treat media coverage as distinct from 'hard' data or statistics about MSV. In fact, as I attempt to show in Chapter 2, most of the public information we have about MSV – including statistics and media coverage – are stories. The data we have about MSV is limited and largely shaped by political choices about what, how, and when to collect and publish information about the phenomena. Incident numbers and survey data do not provide a clear and objective sense of the problem; rather, they tell a story of political and institutional choices, actions, and inaction. Media coverage is a rich resource because it includes and features a number of story tellers, including official responses by military and political leaders, some victim testimony, expert commentary, and opinion pieces. I argue that these converge and make it possible to observe general trends in how the public makes sense of MSV over time.

The first major finding of the research is the political responses and public attention to MSV is largely driven by media coverage of high-profile cases, sometimes understood as 'scandals.' Chapter 2 shows how, in each case country, media attention to MSV ebbs and flows dramatically, with most coverage focused on a select few cases. This chapter also demonstrated how these high-profile cases evoked political responses, including in the form of zero tolerance statements and calls for reviews and/or policy changes. This work reaffirms the significance of media coverage in shaping public conversations and political responses to the problem.

The second set of findings were that there are a number of narratives consistent within media coverage of MSV in each country. Through the case chapters, I highlight the unique stories told consistently in media coverage of MSV. The goal of this analysis was not to identify stories or myths to prove them wrong, or 'debunk' them. Instead, the objective was to identify the stories we tell about MSV and consider how these stories may close out space for alternative ways of making sense of MSV and may inhibit action or systemic change that could reduce MSV. In addition to identifying stories unique to each case country, I found three stories that were consistent across media coverage in all cases. In Chapter 7, I illustrate how these stories converge as forms of institutional gaslighting that undermine efforts to draw attention to MSV or enact systemic change to address the problem and also reify the military as a disciplined and honourable institution.

A third major set of findings related to rhetorical tools. During the research, I noticed several patterns to the use of language in media coverage that were not complete narratives but were also more than just 'themes.' I use the term rhetorical tool to describe several of these patterned language uses that I argue are aimed at convincing or sending specific messages about MSV. I argue that the rhetorical tools and narratives converge in a single message of justified inaction related to MSV. Despite the variations in narratives and rhetorical tools, the overarching message is that nothing can or should be done to address MSV – either because it is already effectively being addressed, the public do not fully understand the problem, or it ultimately is an inevitable outcome of 'good' military training and work. Moreover, the narratives and rhetorical tools I identify not only illuminate how MSV is normalized to a public audience, but also how MSV is framed as an inevitable, if unfortunate, part of 'good' militaries.

Military exceptionalism and institutional gaslighting are useful in understanding these narratives and rhetorical tools and the implications of how we talk about MSV. Military exceptionalism, and deeply held beliefs about 'good' militaries and soldiers, is at the core of narratives that rationalize, legitimize, and distract from MSV. The concept of institutional gaslighting is useful in illustrating how narratives of MSV can diminish, delegitimize, and denigrate any efforts to raise attention to MSV as a systemic issue or suggest ways to address it. I argue that the way we talk about MSV undermines, calls into question, or denies claims that MSV is a systemic issue and reifies the military as a trusted public institution. In doing so, the way we talk about MSV resists and undermines efforts to enact systemic change.

Military sexual violence is not simply a 'military problem'; studying MSV is important not only because MSV is a form of violence that deeply impacts victims, but also because the stories we tell about MSV reveal powerful social beliefs about militarism, gender, sexism, and national identity. Understanding how we talk about MSV can help with broader efforts to understand and dismantle rape culture.

The ultimate purpose of drawing attention to how we talk about MSV, including the related rape myths, tropes, and consistent narratives, is to create space for change and alternative ways of talking about and addressing MSV. This book therefore contributes to broader efforts to shift public narratives about militaries with the ultimate goal of radically reforming these institutions and their roles nationally and internationally.

Bibliography

Abcarian, R. (1992) 'Needed: less than "Zero Tolerance" of harassment', *Los Angeles Times*, 11 August.

Alexopoulos, C. and Siefkes-Andrew, A. J. (2018) 'Framing blame in sexual assault: An analysis of attribution in news stories about sexual assault on college campuses', *Violence against Women*, 25(6), pp. 743–762.

Alleslev, L. and Lui, A. (2015) 'Want to stop sexual assault in the military? Promote women to senior ranks', *The Toronto Star*, 24 June.

Anderssen, E. (1998) 'Murder, sexual-assault cases may be heard by military courts Commons considers legislation to give courts-martial jurisdiction', *The Globe and Mail*, 29 May.

Andrews, D. J., Connor, J., and Wadham, B. (2019) 'The military scandal: Its definition, dynamics, and significance', *Armed Forces & Society*, 46(4), pp. 716–734.

Andrews, D. J., Connor, J., and Wadham, B. (2020) 'The military scandal: its definition, dynamics, and significance', *Armed Forces & Society*, 46(4), pp. 716–734.

The Australian (2011) 'A culture of abuse that has not changed in 20 years', *The Australian*, 9 April.

The Australian (2011) 'Anonymous (former cadet): A culture of abuse that has not changed in 20 years', The Australian, 9 April.

Australian Human Rights Commission (2012) *Review into the Treatment of Women in the Australian Defence Force*. Phase 2 Report.

Australian Human Rights Commission (2013) Australian Human Rights Commission.

Australian Parliament (1994) 'Estimates report/Senate Legislation Committee on Foreign Affairs, Defence and Trade'.

Barno, D. and Bensahel, N. (2020) 'Reflections on the curse of racism in the U.S. Military', War on the Rocks, 30 June.

Becker, E. (2000) 'Women in military say silence on harassment protects careers', *New York Times*, 12 May.

Bell, K., Stein, S., and Hurley, R. (2017) 'When public institutions betray women: News coverage of military sexual violence against women 1991–2013', *Journal of Interdisciplinary Feminist Thought*, 10(1), Article 1.

Bell, W. (1992a) 'Books are to be read', *USA Today*, 28 September.

Benedict, H. (1992) *Virgin or Vamp: How the Press Covers Sex Crimes.* Oxford University Press.

Benedict, H. (1993) *Virgin or Vamp: How the Press Covers Sex Crimes.* Oxford University Press.

Bennett, J. (2013) 'Obama signs sequestration delay, Defense Bill', *Army Times.* Available at: www.armytimes.com/news/2013/01/dn-obama-signs-sequestration-defense-010313.

Bercuson, D. (2015) 'Military leaders must move fast to address "sexualized culture"; In a liberal democratic country, alienating the public is a major threat to national security', *The Globe and Mail*, 4 May.

Berenstain, N. (2020) 'White feminist gaslighting', *Hypatia*, 35(4), pp. 733–758. https://doi.org/10.1017/hyp.2020.31.

Berger, J. (1994) *New York Times*, 1 November.

Blatchford, C. (2015) 'Armed Forces need a total culture shift', *Vancouver Sun*, 2 May.

Blatchford, C. (2015) 'Troubling report blasts military; Inflammatory: Former judge finds mirror stories in Maclean's and L'actualite, without names', Vancouver Sun, 1 May.

Boal, M. (2011) 'The kill team: How U.S. soldiers in Afghanistan murdered innocent civilians', *Rolling Stone*, 28 March. Available at: www.rollingstone.com/politics/politics-news/the-kill-team-how-u-s-soldiers-in-afghanistan-murdered-innocent-civilians-169793/.

Bolan, K. (1992) 'Fed up fighting harassment, corporal quits', *The Toronto Star*, 29 October.

Bond, R. M. (1993) 'The civilian old salt who took on the Navy's Cover-up of Tailhook', *New York Times*, 16 May.

Bornemeier, J. and Morrison, P. (1993) 'Air Force sex harassment case spans years, globe', *Los Angeles Times*, 22 June.

Bostock, D. J. and Daley, J. G. (2007) 'Lifetime and current sexual assault and harassment victimization rates of active-duty United States Air Force women', *Violence Against Women*, 13(9), pp. 927–944.

Boutilier, A. (2015) 'MP Christine Moore faced military harassment first hand', *The Toronto Star*, 30 April.

Box, D. (2014) 'Troops defy orders as girls go topless', *The Australian*, 3 November.

Bradshaw, P. (2014) 'The invisible war review – "Rape in the US Military Is a Secret Epidemic"', *The Guardian*, 6 March. Available at: www.theguardian.com/film/2014/mar/06/the-invisible-war-review-rape-military.

Bridges, T. and Pascoe, J. (2014) 'Hybrid masculinities: new directions in the sociology of men and masculinities', *Sociology Compass*, 8(3), pp. 246–258.

Brito, C. (2020) 'Reward for missing Fort Hood soldier Vanessa Guillen doubles to $50,000.', *CBS News*, 17 June. Available at: www.cbsnews.com/news/vanessa-guillen-missing-fort-hood-soldier-50000-reward/.

Broder, J. and Abrahamson, A. (1992) 'Navy to undergo training to end sex harassment', *Los Angeles Times*, 4 July.

Brook, T. V. (2017) 'Bad Santa: Navy's top admiral kept spokesman after boozy party, sexual predator warning', USA Today, 7 September.

Brownstone, L. M., Holliman, B. D., Gerber, H. R., and Monteith, L. L. (2018) 'The phenomenology of military sexual trauma among women veterans', *Psychology of Men & Masculinities*, 20(1), pp. 115–127.

Burt, M. (1980) 'Cultural myths and supports for rape', *Journal of Personality and Social Psychology*, 38(2), pp. 217–30.

Canadian Press (1998) 'Women under gun in military: magazine', *The Globe and Mail*, 19 May.

Carlton, M. (2011) 'The truth behind sex, lies and Skype', The Sydney Morning Herald, 16 April.

Carreiras, H. (2006) 'Gender and the military. Women in the armed forces of western democracies', *Cass Military Studies*. Routledge [Preprint].

Carson, V. (2002) 'Island bar turns sailors wild', *The Australian*, 11 January.

CNN (2003) 'Air Force officials charge cadet with rape', 14 May.

Collins, P. H. (2000) *Black Feminist Thought: Knowledge, Consciousness, and The Politics of Empowerment*. New York: Routledge.

Collins, P. H. (2002) *Black Feminist Thought: Knowledge, Consciousness, and the Politics of Empowerment*. New York: Routledge.

Collins, P. H. (2008) *Black Feminist Thought: Knowledge, Consciousness, and the Politics of Empowerment*. Routledge.

Connolly, A. (2021) 'Military sexual misconduct class action claims soar to 13,500 as deadline nears', Global News, 8 November.

Courier Mail (1998) 'Booze youth and bad bosses fuel military sex attacks', 12 May.

Crosbie, T. and Sass, J. (2016) 'Governance by scandal? Eradicating sexual assault in the US military', *Politics*, 37(2), pp. 117–133.

Daly, M. (1994a) 'Too much trauma – Navy rape-case doctor', *The Age*, 13 August.

Daly, M. (1994b) 'Too much trauma – Navy rape-case doctor', *The Age*, 13 August.

Daniel, L. (2012) *Panetta, Dempsey Announce Initiatives to Stop Sexual Assault*. American Forces Press Services. Available at: http://archive.defense.gov/news/newsarticle.aspx?id=67954.

Dao, J. (2012) 'Air Force Instructor sentenced to 20 years in sexual assaults', *New York Times*, 21 July. Available at: www.nytimes.com/2012/07/22/us/air-force-instructor-sentenced-to-20-years-in-sex-assaults.html.

DART (2016) *Final Report*. Barton: Defence Abuse Response Taskforce.

Davis, G. and Khonach, T. (2020) 'The paradox of positionality: avoiding, embracing, or resisting feminist accountability', *Fat Studies: An Interdisciplinary Journal of Body Weight and Society*, 9(2), pp. 101–113.

Delacourt, S. (1993) 'Harassment common in Forces, study finds Nearly one in three women and men report encountering difficulties', The Globe and Mail, 6 May.

Dore, C. (1999) 'Ancient art gives military a gentle nudge into new age', *The Australian*, 23 February.

Du Mont, J. and Parnis, D. (1999) 'Judging women: The pernicious effects of rape mythology', *Canadian Woman Studies* [Preprint].

Duncanson, C. (2013) *Forces for Good? Military Masculinities and Peacebuilding in Afghanistan and Iraq*. Palgrave Macmillan.

Duriesmith, D. (2017) *Masculinity and New War: The Gendered Dynamics of Contemporary Armed Conflict*. Routledge.

Easteal, P., Holland, K., and Judd, K. (2015) 'Enduring themes and silences in media portrayals of violence against women', *Women's Studies International Forum*, 48(1), pp. 103–113. https://doi.org/10.1016/j .wsif.2014.10.015.

Eichler, M. (2014) 'Militarized masculinities in international relations', *The Brown Journal of World Affairs*, 21(1), pp. 81–93.

Encloe, C. (2011) 'The mundane matters', *International Political Sociology*, 5(4), pp. 447–450.

Entman, R. M. (1993) 'Framing: Toward clarification of a fractured paradigm', *Journal of Communication*, 43, pp. 51–58.

Erlandson, R. (1996) 'Captain saw Army as "a way up" from rural poverty acquaintances puzzle over charges against a man "so straight"', *Baltimore Sun*, 19 November. Available at: www.baltimoresun.com/news/bs-xpm- 1996-11-19-1996324001-story.html.

Finch, E. and Munro, V. E. (2004) 'Juror stereotypes and blame attribution in rape cases involving intoxicants: The findings of a pilot study', *The British Journal of Criminology*, 45(1), pp. 25–38. https://doi.org/10.1093/ bjc/azh055.

Fiore, F. and Kelly, D. (2003) 'Sky was limit for cadet, until her harassment complaint', *Los Angeles Times*, 12 March. Available at: www.latimes .com/archives/la-xpm-2003-mar-12-na-academy12-story.html.

Firestone, J. M. and Harris, R. J. (2009) 'Sexual harassment in the U. S. military reserve component: A preliminary analysis', *Armed Forces & Society*, 36(1), pp. 86–102.

Fitzgibbon, J. (2012) 'Bring Defence to Heel', *The Australian,* 13 July.

Fortin, J. (2017) 'Fort Benning drill sergeants suspended amid sexual mis- conduct allegations', *New York Times,* 23 August. Available at: www .nytimes.com/2017/08/23/us/fort-benning-sexual-assault.html.

Francis, D. (2013) 'Military sexual assaults cost more than $872 million', *The Fiscal Times*, 30 April.

Fuller, A. (1993) 'COVER STORY sex and the military: Battling harass- ment', The Globe and Mail, 7 August.

Furedi, F. (2012) 'Band of brothers' under fire', The Australian, 17 March.

Gallant, J. (2021) 'Almost 19,000 claims submitted in Canadian military sexual misconduct lawsuits', *Toronto Star*, 25 November.

Galloway, G. (2015) 'Assault victims sought legal protection from military college dismissal: lawyer; Victims of sexual assault sought legal protection to prevent military college from disciplining and dismissing them', The Globe and Mail, 30 April.

Garrett, L. (1992) 'Harassment most ugly', *Los Angeles Times*, 27 June.

Goldman, J. J. (1997) 'Cadet says classmate raped, stalked her; Military; West Point investigators call incident consensual. Detective hired by student's lawyer raises questions about academy's handling of case', Los Angeles Times, 15 April.

Government of Canada (2021) *DAOD 9005-1, Sexual Misconduct Response.*

Gray, J., Cernetig, M., Philp, M., Ha, T. T., Appleby, T. (1997) 'Sexism remains problem in army Women cite harassment cases', The Globe and Mail, 1 January.

Greene, G. (1998) 'Officers and gentlemen?', *The Age*, 12 June.

Griffin, S. (1992) 'In USA, military training faulted for some violence', *USA Today*, 7 October.

Gross, J. (1993a) 'Oct. 3–9: Tailhook '93; An Admiral is salvaged as the fraternity sobers up', *New York Times*, 10 October.

Gross, J. (1993b) 'Tailhook gathering is a far cry from the last one', *New York Times*, 10 October.

Guillen, G. (2021) *Free Speech Radio*. KPFA FM.

Hale, C. and Matt, M. (2019) 'The intersection of race and rape viewed through the prism of a modern-day emmett till', *American Bar Association* [Preprint].

Hall, B. and Ireland, J. (2012) 'Sex offenders may hold senior posts, says defence report', *Sydney Morning Herald*, 11 July.

Hannay, C. (2015) 'Why victims of sexual harassment or assault in the military stay silent; A review into sexual misconduct in the Canadian Armed Forces cited impact on career, privacy and lack of trust as reasons most incidents are never reported', *The Globe and Mail*, 30 April.

Healy, H. (1998) 'NEWS ANALYSIS; Army verdict could stifle female soldiers', *Los Angeles Times*, 15 March.

Healy, H. and Reza, H. G. (1992) 'Pentagon blasts Navy's Tailhook investigation', *Los Angeles Times*, 25 September.

Healy, H. and Reza, H. G. (1993) 'Tailhook probe finds lurid cases of sexual misconduct', *Los Angeles Times*, 6 February.

Healy, M. (1992) 'New plans offered to fight sexual harassment in Navy', *Los Angeles Times*, 18 September.

Healy, M. (1993) '140 Officers faulted in Tailhook sex scandal', *Los Angeles Times*, 24 April.

Healy, M. (1998) 'NEWS ANALYSIS; Army verdict could stifle female soldiers', Los Angeles Times, 15 March.

Healy, M. and Reza, H. G. (1992) 'Pentagon blasts Navy's tailhook investigation', Los Angeles Times, 25 September.

Healy, M. and Reza, H. G. (1993) 'Tailhook probe finds lurid cases of sexual misconduct', Los Angeles Times, 6 February.

Hendren, J. (2003) 'The nation; Decision on Army secretary on hold as assault inquiry continues; Senate panel stalls the nomination of James Roche pending the results of a probe into sexual abuse at the Air Force Academy', Los Angeles Times, 1 October.

Hennigan, W. J. (2014) 'Military sex assaults persist; reported incidents rise 8% in the last year. The Pentagon plans new prevention efforts and more', *Los Angeles Times*, 5 December.

Higate, P. (2012) 'Drinking Vodka from the "Butt-Crack"', *International Feminist Journal of Politics*, 14(4), pp. 450–469, https://doi.org/10.1080/14616742.2012.726092

Hollander, J. (2015) 'Good guys don't rape: gender, domination, and mobilizing rape', *Gender & Society*, 30(1).

Hooks, B. (2000) *Feminism Is for Everybody: Passionate Politics*. Cambridge, MA: South End Press.

Hordge-Freeman, E. (2018) '"Bringing your whole self to research": The power of the researcher's body, emotions, and identities in ethnography', *International Journal of Qualitative Methods*, 17, pp. 1–9.

Jackson, R. L. and Freeman, D. (1998) 'McKinney demoted, reprimanded by Army; Court-martial: he will retire one pay grade below Sergeant Major, costing him $875 a month in pension benefits. Accusers say they've paid higher price', *Los Angeles Times*, 17 March.

James, N. (2012) 'Should there be a royal commission into the ADF?', *The Sydney Morning Herald*, 14 July. Available at: www.smh.com.au/politics/federal/should-there-be-a-royal-commission-into-the-adf-20120713-221of.html (Accessed: 18 September 2018).

Jane, E. (2011) 'Digital sexual revolution leaves a lot to be desired', *The Australian*, 16 April.

Janofsky, M. (2003a) 'Air Force begins an inquiry of ex-cadets' rape charges', *New York Times*, 20 February.

Janofsky, M. (2003b) 'General asks Air Force to build trust at Academy', New York Times, 21 February.

Johnson, D. (1997) 'A focus on treating all recruits better', New York Times, 17 March.

Jolidon, L. (1992a) 'Incidents trigger calls for investigative reform', *USA Today*, 25 September.

Jolidon, L. (1992b) 'Navy orders outside probe of pilot scandal', *USA Today*, 19 June.

Jolidon, L. (1992c) 'Scandal sets navy adrift / acting secretary named to navigate into '90s / harassment is on the front burner', *USA Today*, 8 July.

Jones, A. (2012) 'Abuse in the military: running with a pack of wolves', *ABC*, 22 January.

Kasinsky, R. G. (1998) 'Tailhook and the construction of sexual harassment in the media: "rowdy navy boys" and women who made a difference', *SAGE* [Preprint].

Kearney, S. (2005) 'Navy leads in bad behaviour', The Australian, 30 November.

Kelly, D. (2003) 'The Nation; Air Force "will not tolerate" sexual assaults, cadet told; secretary vows to remove "criminals" after more than 20 women say academy's brass ignored their reports of rape or threatened retaliation', *Los Angeles Times*, 28 February.

Kennedy-Cuomo, M. (2019) 'Institutional gaslighting: Investigations to silence the victim and protect the perp', *Brown Political Review* [Preprint].

Kilborn, P. T. (1997) '5 women say sex charges in Army case were coerced', *New York Times*, 12 March.

Kimerling, R., Street, A. E., Pavao, J., et al. (2010) 'Military-related sexual trauma among veterans health administration patients returning from Afghanistan and Iraq', *American Journal of Public Health*, 100(8), pp. 1409–1412.

Knaus, C. and Inman, M. (2013) 'ADFA Skype scandal cadets sentenced, avoid jail', *The Sydney Morning Herald*, 23 October. Available at: www.smh.com.au/national/act/adfa-skype-scandal-cadets-sentenced-avoid-jail-20131023-2w0hz.html (Accessed: 16 January 2019).

Komarow, S. (1996) 'Army expands sex abuse investigation', *USA Today*, 1 November.

Krauss, C. (1997) 'Tough line by Secretary of Defense', New York Times, 1 February.

Kube, C. and Connor, T. (2013) 'Fort Benning drill sergeants suspended for alleged sexual misconduct.', *NBC News*, 23 August. Available at: www.nbcnews.com/news/us-news/fort-benning-drill-sergeants-suspended-alleged-sexual-misconduct-n795186.

Lalonde, J. (2020) *Resilience Is Futile: The Life and Death and Life of Julie Lalonde*. Toronto: Between the Lines.

Lancaster, J. (1993) 'Tailhook probe implicates 140 officers', *The Washington Post*, 24 April. Available at: www.washingtonpost.com/archive/politics/1993/04/24/tailhook-probe-implicates-140-officers/e004554a-0440-4371-b8a9-a2ecaad05785/.

Lawrence, C. (2012) '31 victims identified in widening Air Force sex scandal', *CNN*, 29 June. Available at: www.cnn.com/2012/06/28/justice/texas-air-force-scandal.

Lewis, N. A. (1992) 'President meets female officer in Navy incident', *New York Times*, 28 June.

Lonsway, K. A. and Fitzgerald, L. F. (1994) 'Rape Myths', *Psychology of Women Quarterly*, 18(2), pp. 133–164.

Los Angeles Times (1992) 'Harassment Most Ugly', 27 June.

MacKenzie, M. H. (2015) *Beyond the Band of Brothers*. Cambridge University Press.

MacKenzie, M., Gunaydin, E., and Chaudhuri, U. (2020) 'Illicit military behavior as exceptional and inevitable: Media coverage of military sexual violence and the "bad apples" paradox', *International Studies Quarterly*, 64(1), pp. 45–56.

Mahler, J. and Rutenburg, J. (2019) 'How Rupert Murdoch's Empire of Influence Remade the World', *New York Times Magazine*, 3 April.

Marzolf, M. T. (1993) 'Deciding what's "women's news."', *Media Studies Journal*, 7(1 & 2), pp. 33–47.

Mason, C. (2005) 'The hillbilly defense: Culturally mediating U.S. terror at home and abroad', *Indiana University Press*, 17(3), pp. 39–63.

Matthews, M., Morral, A. R., Schell, T. L., et al. (2021) *Organizational Characteristics Associated with Risk of Sexual Assault and Sexual Harassment in the U.S. Army*. Santa Monica, CA: RAND Corporation. www.rand.org/pubs/research_reports/RRA1013-1.html.

McGuire, D. L. (2011) *At the Dark End of the Street: Black Women, Rape, and Resistance – a New History of the Civil Rights Movement from Rosa Parks to the Rise of Black Power*. New York: Knopf Doubleday Publishing Group.

Mesok, E. (2016) 'Sexual violence and the US military: Feminism, US empire, and the failure of liberal equality', *Feminist Studies*, 42(1), pp. 41–69.

Meyers, M. (2017) 'Army fires infantry basic training battalion commander', *Army Times*, 25 September. Available at: www.defensenews.com/news/your-army/2017/09/25/army-fires-infantry-basic-training-battalion-commander/.

Middleton, K. (1994) 'Sex commissioner hits ADF report', *The Age*, 26 August.

Millar, K. M. and Tidy, J. (2017) 'Combat as a moving target: Masculinities, the heroic soldier myth and normative martial violence', *Critical Military Studies* [Preprint].

Milloy, C. (1997) 'Aberdeen's other scandal', *Washington Post*, 4 May. Available at: www.washingtonpost.com/archive/local/1997/05/04/aberdeens-other-scandal/b0ee4e30-b87e-4e66-9e24-50faee9d9ac7/.

Mitchell, B. (2000) 'Sailors sue over going to sea', *The Australian*, 8 March.

Molotsky, I. (1996) 'Troubles at Naval Academy result in restricted privileges', *New York Times*, 17 April.

Morris, M. (1995) 'By force of arms: Rape, war, and military culture', *Duke Law Journal*, 45(4), p. 651.

Morris, M. (1996) 'By force of arms: Rape, war, and military culture', *Duke Law Journal*, 45(4), pp. 651–781.

Mulrine, A. (2012) 'Pentagon report: Sexual assault in the military up dramatically – CSMonitor.com', *CS Monitor*, 19 January. Available at: www.csmonitor.com/USA/Military/2012/0119/Pentagon-report-Sexual-assault-in-the-military-up-dramatically (Accessed: 29 July 2019).

Murray, M. (1998) 'New training bids to cut harassment Officer points to special lessons all ranks must take', The Toronto Star, 20 May.

Myers, S. L. (2000) 'Personnel File of General Bore No Hint of Harassment', New York Times, 7 April.

National Defence (2022) Training and educational materials about sexual misconduct. Government of Canada.

The National Resource Center on Domestic Violence (2022) *Military Sexual Trauma (MST)*. Available at: https://vawnet.org/sc/military-sexual-trauma-mst.

Neiberg, M. and Schlossman, S. (1997) 'THE MILITARY; The problem that won't go away', Los Angeles Times, 28 December.

New York Times (1993a) 'Admiral Kelso keeps his command', Editorial, 6 October.

New York Times (1993b) 'Officers and gentlemen? Hardly.', Editorial, 26 April.

New York Times (2003) 'The Air Force Academy Scandal', 8 March. Available at: www.nytimes.com/2003/03/08/opinion/the-air-force-academy-scandal.html.

New York Times (2012) 'Air Force Instructor Sentenced to 20 Years in Sexual Assaults', 21 July. By the Associated Press. Available at: www.nytimes.com/2012/07/22/us/air-force-instructor- sentenced-to-20-years-in-sex-assaults.html.

Nicholson, B. (2011) 'Warship's "bullet-proof" engineers blamed for sexual misconduct', The Australian, 22 February.

Nicholson, B. and Dodd, M. (2011) 'Sex, betrayal and a scapegoat', *The Australian*, 8 April.

Noble, K. B. (1994) 'Closing arguments in Tailhook lawsuit', *New York Times*, 28 October.

O'Connor, J. (2020) 'Murdoch empire "an arrogant cancer on democracy": Rudd', *Independent*, 11 October.

O'Keefe, S. (1993) 'On Tailhook, drop the other shoe', *Los Angeles Times*, 28 February.

Oppel, N. (2014) 'Emails show shared concern of false testimony in Army sexual assault case', *New York Times*, 10 March.

Owens, J. (2011) 'ADF culture blamed for backflip on abuse', *The Austra-lian*, 30 November.

Pearce, D., McKean, M., and Rumble, G. A. (2012) Report of the review of allegations of sexual and other abuse in Defence. Available at: https://apo.org.au/node/28544.

Perry, T. (2000) 'California and the West; Navy renews relations with Tail-hook Assn.; Military: the action ends eight years of estrangement after notorious convention in Las Vegas', *Los Angeles Times*, 20 January.

Phillips, D. (2021) 'Military missteps allowed soldier accused of murder to flee, report says', *New York Times*, 30 April. Available at: www.nytimes .com/2021/04/30/us/vanessa-guillen-fort-hood-aaron-robinson.html.

Ramsey, A. (1994) 'Ungentlemantly conduct in the services', *Sydney Morn-ing Herald*, 9 July.

Razack, S. (2004) *Dark Threats and White Knights: The Somalia Affair, Peacekeeping, and the New Imperialism*. University of Toronto Press.

Razack, S. H. (2016) 'Sexualized violence and colonialism: Reflections on the Inquiry into missing and murdered indigenous women', *Canadian Journal of Women and Law*, 28(2), pp. i–iv.

Reay, D. (1996) 'Dealing with difficult differences: reflexivity and social class in feminist research', *Feminist & Psychology*, 6(3), pp. 443–456.

Rhode, D. L. (1995) 'Media images, feminist issues', *Signs*, 20(3), pp. 685–710.

Richter, P. (1997) 'Drill sergeant guilty of 18 charges of rape; Army: He is also convicted on 25 other counts. Case is considered key in Military's sexual misconduct scandal', *Los Angeles Times*, 30 April.

Richter, P. (1998) 'General retired despite sex Allegations; Military: Army chief of staff permitted honorable retirement while sexual misconduct investigation was pending. Defense chief calls for review', *Los Angeles Times*, 28 March.

Richter, P. (2000a) 'Accused general is nominee for No. 2 job; Military: Pentagon says officer was selected for investigative post after allegation of inappropraite sexual conduct. But he has been given temporary

Richter, P. (2000b) 'Colleague had sexually harassed female general, amy concludes; Military: Inspector believes Maj. Gen. Kennedy, The service's highest-ranking woman, was Grabbed and Kissed. Maj. Gen. Larry Smith Says He Will Retire', *Los Angeles Times*, 14 July.

Richter, P. and Kempster, N. (1997) '"Disgusted" by Hazing, Cohen Calls for "Zero Tolerance"; Military: Marine corps incident prompts criticism from defense chief. But experts say such a battle would be difficult to win', *Los Angeles Times*, 1 February.

Ricks, T. E. (1996) 'U.S. soldiers face charges for harassment', *Wall Street Journal*, 11 November.

Rico, A. (2017) 'Why military women are missing from the #MeToo Movement', *Time Magazine*, 12 December.

Risen, J. (2013a) 'Air force leaders testify on culture that led to sexual assaults of recruits', *New York Times,* 23 January. Available at: www.nytimes.com/2013/01/24/us/air-force-leaders-testify-on-culture-that-led-to-sexual-assaults-of-recruits.html.

Risen, J. (2013b) 'Former air force recruit speaks out about rape by her Sergeant at Lackland', *The New York Times*, 26 February. Available at: www.nytimes.com/2013/02/27/us/former-air-force-recruit-speaks-out-about-rape-by-her-sergeant-at-lackland.html (Accessed: 12 May 2014).

Ross, R. and Stone, L. (1992) 'Navy base bears brunt of Tailhook scandal', *USA Today*, 5 August.

Ruíz, E. (2020) 'Cultural gaslighting', *Hypatia*, 35(4), pp. 687–713.

Sadler, A., Cheney, A., Mendeling, M., et al., (2022) 'Servicemen's perceptions of male sexual assault and barriers to reporting during active component and reserve/national guard military service', *Journal of Interpersonal Violence*, 36(7–8) online only pp. NP3596–NP3623.

Sallot, J. (1998) 'Sex harassment must stop, top general warns troops Baril reads riot act to "thugs and brutes" in Canadian military', *The Globe and Mail*, 15 July.

Sampert, S. (2010) 'Let me tell you a story: English–Canadian newspapers and sexual assault myths', *Canadian Journal of Women and the Law* [Preprint]. https://doi.org/10.3138/cjwl.22.2.301.

Scheufele, D. A. and Tewksbury, D. (2006) 'Framing, agenda setting, and priming: The evolution of three media effects models', *Journal of Communication*, 57(1), pp. 9–20.

Schmitt, E. (1990a) '1 out of 3 women in military study report sexual harassment incidents', *New York Times*, 12 September.

Schmitt, E. (1990b) '990 Are graduated at Naval Academy', *New York Times*, 31 May.

Schmitt, E. (1992a) 'Navy Chief seeks anti-harassment law', *New York Times*, 3 July.

Schmitt, E. (1992b) 'The military has a lot to learn about women', *New York Times*, 2 August.

Schmitt, E. (1992c) 'Wall of silence impedes inquiry into a rowdy Navy convention', *New York*.

Schmitt, E. (1994a) 'Navy women bringing new era on carriers', *New York Times*, 21 February.

Schmitt, E. (1994b) 'Retired admiral assails senator over sex harassment complaint', *New York Times*, 4 November.

Schmitt, E. (1995) 'Study says sexual harassment persists at Military Academies', *New York Times*, 5 April.

Schmitt, E. (1996) 'War is Hell. So is regulating sex', *New York Times*, 17 November.

Sciolino, E. (1997) 'Sergeant convicted of 18 counts of raping female subordinates', *New York Times*, 30 April.

Sendén, M. G., Lindholm, T., and Sikström, S. (2014) 'Biases in news media as reflected by personal pronouns in evaluative contexts', *Social Psychology*, 45(2), pp. 103–111.

Shadley, R. (2016) '20 years on, what the army's learned from the Aberdeen sex scandal', *Army Times*, 8 November. Available at: www.armytimes .com/opinion/2016/11/08/20-years-on-what-the-army-s-learned-from-the-aberdeen-sex-scandal/.

Shahid, M. (1992) 'Sexual harassment in the military', *USA Today*, 27 May.

Shanker, T. (2013) 'At Navy installation, sexual assault prevention begins at boot camp', *New York Times*, 8 July.

Shaw, J., Campbell, R., Cain, D., and Feeney, H., et al. (2017) 'Beyond surveys and scales: How rape myths manifest in sexual assault police records', *Psychology of Violence*, 7(4), pp. 602–614.

Shenon, P. (1997) 'General reprimanded in scandal at base', *New York Times*, 11 September.

Shepherd, L. J. (2012) *Gender, Violence and Popular Culture: Telling Stories*. Routledge.

Shilts, R. (1994) *Conduct Unbecoming*. Ballantine Books.

Sielke, S. (2002) *Reading Rape: The Rhetoric of Sexual Violence in American Literature and Culture, 1790–1990*. Princeton University Press.

Silverman, A. (2020) 'A reason for the rampage: Aggrieved entitlement and white masculinities', Sociology Senior Seminar Papers. 62. https:// creativematter.skidmore.edu/socio_stu_stu_schol/62.

Simon, R. (1990) 'Act of harassment betrays the ideal of military honor', *Los Angeles Times*, 20 May.

Snow, D. (2011) 'ADF no school for scandal: Houston', *Sydney Morning Herald*, 9 April.

Snow, D. (2012a) 'Battle to reform military culture', Sydney Morning Herald, 25 August.

Snow, D. (2012b) 'There will be women in foxholes', Sydney Morning Herald, 7 January.

Solnit, R. (2014) *Men Explain Things to Me*. Haymarket Books.

Stavrakakis, Y. (2007) *The Lacanian Left: Psychoanalysis, Theory, and Politics*. SUNY Press.

Stayner, T. (2022) 'Sexual assault complaints in Australian Defence Force soar to eight-year high', SBS News, 21 October.

Stone, A. (1992a) 'At VA, tales of harassment/Women fear for their jobs', *USA Today*, 1 August.

Stone, A. (1992b) 'Tailhook could be agent of change', *USA Today*, 30 July.

Stone, A. (1992c) 'Women in military: Sex harassment and silence', 23 July.

Stone, A. (1997) 'Army sex accuser puts conditions on her testimony', *USA Today*, 9 July.

Stone, A. (1998a) 'McKinney jury meets today to decide sentence', *USA Today*, 16 March.

Stone, A. (1998b) 'Military's gender battle still far from resolved', *USA Today*, 1 March.

Stone, A. and Komarow, L. (1998) 'McKinney reprimanded, loses rank', *USA Today*, 17 March.

Street, A. E., Stafford, J., Mahan, C. M., Hendricks, A., et al. (2008) 'Sexual harassment and assault experienced by reservists during military service: prevalence and health correlates', *Journal of Rehabilitation Research and Development*, 45(3), pp. 409–420.

Suro, R. (1991) 'Texas A&M cadets charge sex abuse', *New York Times*, 7 October.

Sweet, P. (2019) 'The sociology of gaslighting', *American Sociological Review*, 84(5), pp. 851–875.

The Sydney Morning Herald (1998) 'Indiscipline', Editorial, 12 June.

The Sydney Morning Herald (2012) 'Defence stuck in its own mud', Editorial, 16 June.

Thakker, J. and Durrant, R. (2006) 'News coverage of sexual offending in New Zealand, 2003', *New Zealand Journal of Psychology*, 35(1), pp. 28–35.

Thompson, A. (1998) 'Back in the hot seat…'I'm calm and cool,' says Defence Minister Art Eggleton as he handles the military sex scandal – and his marriage breakup', *The Toronto Star*, 4 August.

Thompson, A. (1998) 'General admits sexual abuse exists in military rules out inquiry saying problem is not widespread.', *The Toronto Star*, 20 May.

Thompson, A. (1998) 'Military recruiting style under fire Forces' selection process doesn't pass muster, critics say', *The Toronto Star*, 19 July.

Thomsen, C. J., Stander, V. A., Foster, R. E., Gallus, J. A. (2017) 'Understanding and Addressing Sexual Harassment and Sexual Assault in the US Military', In: Bowles, S., Bartone, P. (eds). *Handbook of Military Psychology*, Cham: Springer, pp. 357–373.

Thomson, G. (2012) 'Smith a resolute example for Defence Force', *The Sydney Morning Herald*, 9 March. Available at: www.smh.com.au/politics/federal/smith-a-resolute-example-for-defence-force-20120308-1uneb.html (Accessed: 18 September 2018).

Titunik, R. F. (2000) 'The first wave: Gender integration and military culture', *Armed Forces & Society*, 26(2), pp. 229–257. https://doi.org/10.1177/0095327X0002600204.

Titunik, R. F. (2008) 'The Myth of the Macho Military', *Polity*, 40(2), pp. 137–163.

The Toronto Star (1993) 'Tory minister tells female MP to quiet down, stop yapping', 20 March.

The Toronto Star (1998) 'More sex abuse reports emerge in wake of article Defence minister calls behaviour "unacceptable"', Editorial, 25 May.

Toronto Star (1998) 'Tough line needed on abuse in military', Editorial, 22 May.

The Toronto Star (1999) 'Eggleton buffs military's reputation', Editorial, 11 December.

The Toronto Star (2000) 'Spousal abuse: The military's top challenge', Editorial, 14 May.

The Toronto Star (2015a) 'Canada's military needs an about-face on sexual misconduct', Editorial, 30 April.

The Toronto Star (2015b) 'Gen. Vance's search-and-destroy mission targets sexual misconduct', Editorial, 18 August.

Turner, R. (2015) 'Military making lasting changes – Sexual misconduct will not be tolerated.', Winnipeg Free Press, 9 May.

U.S. Navy's Military Sealift Command (2022) *Sexual Assault Prevention and Response*. Available at: www.msc.usff.navy.mil/Organization/Head-quarters/MSC-SAPR/.

USA Today (1992a) 'Books are to be read', Editorial, 28 September.

USA Today (1992b) 'Military and harassment', Editorial, 21 February.

USA Today (1996) 'Feeding predators', Editorial, 11 November.

USA Today (2003) 'No respect for female cadets', Editorial, 21 February.

Vancouver Sun (2015) 'Armed Forces need a total culture shift', 2 May.

Vandello, J. A., Bosson, J. K., Cohen, D., Burnaford, R. M., and Weaver, J. R. (2008) 'Precarious manhood', *Journal of Personality and Social Psychology*, 95(6), pp. 1325–1339. https://doi.org/10.1037/a0012453.

Wadham, B. (2012) 'Defence Force's great battle within: cleaning up its own act', The Age, 2 March.

Wadham, B. (2013) 'Brotherhood: Homosociality, totality and military subjectivity', *Australian Feminist Studies*, 28(76), pp. 212–235.

Wadham, B. (2017) 'Violence in the Military and Relations Among Men: Military Masculinities and "Rape Prone Cultures"', In: Woodward, R. and Duncanson, C. (eds). *The Palgrave International Handbook of Gender and the Military*. London: Palgrave Macmillan UK, pp. 241–256. https://doi.org/10.1057/978-1-137-51677-0_15.

Wadham, B. and Bridges, D. (2020) 'Gender under fire: portrayals of military women in the Australian print media', *Feminist Media Studies*, 20(2), pp. 219–237.

Wall Street Journal (1992) 'Conduct unbecoming', Editorial, 7 July.

Wall Street Journal (1996) 'This time, don't persecute the innocent', Editorial, 9 December.

Ward, J. (1998) 'Crush sex abuse, top general orders', Winnipeg Free Press, 15 July.

Warner, C. (2014) 'The politics of sex abuse in hierarchies: a comparative study of the Catholic Church and the United States Military', *APSA 2014 Annual Meeting Paper* [Preprint].

Wattie, C. (2015) 'The Armed Forces' war on women needs to stop now; It's not a surprise to learn there is sexism in the Canadian Armed Forces. No one ever expected the military to be a shining light in the battle for gender equality. But it should have at least tried.', The Globe and Mail, 30 April.

Weizel, R. (1997) 'Coast Guard: Working it out the coed way', New York Times, 26 January.

Wertsch, M. E. (1992) 'The pathology is alcohol', Los Angeles Times, 16 August.

Wieskamp, V. (2018) '"I'm going out there and i'm telling this story": Victimhood and empowerment in narratives of military sexual violence', *Western Journal of Communication*, 83 (2), pp. 133–150.

Wilson, C. (2020) 'Australia's defence forces have spent $50 million on sexual abuse claims in the past three years', *Pedestrian Group*, 28 October.

Winerip, M. (2013) 'Revisiting the military's Tailhook scandal', *New York Times*, 13 May. Available at: www.nytimes.com/2013/05/13/booming/revisiting-the-militarys-tailhook-scandal-video.html.

Wood, E. J. and Toppelberg, N. (2017) 'The persistence of sexual assault within the US military', *Journal of Peace Research*, 54(5), pp. 620–633.

Woodford, J. (1998) 'Sexual forces', Sydney Morning Herald, 11 June.

Wrigley, A. (1993) 'No defence for forces that are isolated', *The Age*, 27 September.

York, G. (1993) 'Sex harassment called rampant on military bases Federal report says complaining carries risk of serious harm', *The Globe and Mail*, 11 March.

Young, I. M. (2003) 'The logic of masculinist protection: Reflections on the current security state', *The University of Chicago Press*, 29(1), pp. 1–25.

Index

For EU product safety concerns, contact us at Calle de José Abascal, 56–1°, 28003 Madrid, Spain or eugpsr@cambridge.org.

www.ingramcontent.com/pod-product-compliance
Ingram Content Group UK Ltd.
Pitfield, Milton Keynes, MK11 3LW, UK
UKHW020351140625
459647UK00020B/2399

* 9 7 8 1 0 0 9 2 7 3 9 3 0 *